CONTEMPORARY'S

# Breakthroughs

## in Math

# CONTEMPORARY'S

# Breakthroughs

## in Math

# EXERCISE BOOK

Mc
Graw
Hill   Wright Group

**Wright Group**

ISBN: 0-8092-0932-2

Send all inquiries to:
Wright Group/McGraw-Hill
130 East Randolph Street, Suite 400
Chicago, Illinois 60601

Printed in the United States of America.

9 10 VLP VLP  08

The *McGraw·Hill* Companies

# CONTENTS

# TO THE STUDENT

Welcome to *Breakthroughs in Math Exercise Book*. In this book, you'll be practicing the problem-solving skills you learned in Contemporary's *Breakthroughs in Math Book 1* and *Book 2*. You will practice skills ranging from selecting the necessary information to choosing the correct operation to working multi-step word problems.

Each exercise in this book **corresponds to one or more lessons** in *Breakthroughs in Math Book 1* or *Book 2*. Look for the words "Book 1" or "Book 2" and "Text Pages" in the margin next to each group of problems. These margin notes will tell you in which book and on which pages you can review the skill or skills being used in that group of problems.

You'll find answers to all the exercises at the back of this book. Be sure to check your work at the end of each group of problems before you move on. Keep in mind that there is often more than one way to approach a problem. It's OK if your approach differs from the one shown in the answer key. The important thing is to apply your math reasoning skills and to arrive at the correct solution.

When you are finished with the book, take the Post-Test. The chart on page 64 will help you evaluate the work you have done.

And finally, transfer the problem-solving skills you learn here to the numbers you encounter in real life. The more you explore, the better equipped you'll be to solve the problems that come your way.

# BREAKTHROUGHS IN MATH

## Book 1

# WHOLE NUMBERS

Book 1
**Text Pages**
12–13, 16

## Rounding Whole Numbers and Money

It is often more useful to work with **round numbers** than exact figures.

**Directions:** Round the following numbers to fit the given situations.

John Madden announces NFL football games. During each game, he reports the approximate attendance by rounding the actual attendance figures. What attendance figure would he report for each game listed below?

|  | Actual Attendance | Announced |
|---|---|---|
| **EXAMPLE**  Rams vs. Lions | 60,873 | _61,000_ |
| 1. Bears vs. Colts | 60,519 | _____ |
| 2. Cowboys vs. Giants | 76,410 | _____ |
| 3. Vikings vs. Packers | 57,614 | _____ |
| 4. Buccaneers vs. Falcons | 41,274 | _____ |

Wildlife Alert has been conducting a random count of various wild birds in a selected forest preserve. In the report, it listed the approximate number of each bird. Round the following numbers to be included in the report.

|  | Number Sighted | Number Reported |
|---|---|---|
| 5. sparrows | 628 | _____ |
| 6. crows | 151 | _____ |
| 7. geese | 265 | _____ |
| 8. blackbirds | 907 | _____ |

Prices are often written so that items appear to cost less. Round each price to the approximate cost.

|  | Price | Approximate Cost |
|---|---|---|
| 9. one pound of ground beef | $1.89 | _____ |
| 10. one men's shirt | $28.75 | _____ |
| 11. a used car | $5,995.95 | _____ |
| 12. one month's rent for an apartment | $689.50 | _____ |

**Check your answers on page 65.**

# Writing Dollars and Cents

**Directions:** Complete the checks below to pay JoAnn's rent, electricity, and telephone bills. The amount for each bill is:

- electricity (People's Electricity): $47.53
- rent (Home Management, Inc.): $375.00
- telephone (Tone Telephone): $28.66

---

JoAnn Fellows                **589**
363 Hibernia Dr.
Carroll, MD 21000                _____ 19 __

Pay to the Order of _People's Electricity_    $ _____

_____ Dollars

**Citizens' Bank**

_JoAnn Fellows_

0421873090      444    0999    6    589

---

JoAnn Fellows                **590**
363 Hibernia Dr.
Carroll, MD 21000                _____ 19 __

Pay to the Order of _Home Management, Inc._ $ _____

_____ Dollars

**Citizens' Bank**

_JoAnn Fellows_

0421873090      444    0999    6    590

---

JoAnn Fellows                **591**
363 Hibernia Dr.
Carroll, MD 21000                _____ 19 __

Pay to the Order of _Tone Telephone_    $ _____

_____ Dollars

**Citizens' Bank**

_JoAnn Fellows_

0421873090      444    0999    6    591

---

**Check your answers on page 65.**

# ADDITION SKILLS

Book 1
**Text Pages**
28–31

## Identifying What You Are to Find

The first step in solving a word problem is understanding what you are asked to find. Be sure to read through each problem before beginning.

**Directions:** In each of the following problems, underline what you are asked to find. Then solve and check each problem, showing all your work.

**EXAMPLE**

The 1980 census reported 5,925 people living in Golden City. By 1990, this number had increased by 2,304. <u>What was the population of Golden City in 1990?</u>

| Add | | Check |
|---|---|---|
| 5,925 | (1980 population) | 2,304 |
| + 2,304 | (increase in population) | + 5,925 |
| 8,229 | (1990 population) | 8,229 |

1. The current tuition at Trident Community College of $39.00 per credit hour will be raised $9.00 next semester. How much will tuition be per credit hour next semester?

2. Mark earns $466.00 per week at his full-time job and $123.00 on his weekend job. How much does Mark earn each week?

3. Baltimore is usually 10° warmer than Chicago. What temperature will it probably be in Baltimore when it is 48° in Chicago?

4. The train goes from Harrisburg to Chicago in 14 hours and then from Chicago to Minneapolis in 9 hours. How long does it take this train to travel from Harrisburg to Minneapolis?

5. Charlie put some biscuits in the oven at 15 minutes after 6:00 P.M. If the biscuits take 12 minutes to bake, what time will they be ready?

6. In one month, the Scotts made a car payment of $271.10, spent $113.87 on maintenance, paid an insurance premium of $62.50, and spent $56.60 on gasoline. Find how much it cost the Scotts to own and operate the car that month.

**Check your answers on page 65.**

# Finding Necessary Information

The second step in solving word problems is deciding what information is needed to answer the question.

**Directions:** All the problems on this page refer to the menu pictured. For each problem, list the necessary information and solve the problem.

| **Appetizers** | **Sandwiches** | **Beverages** |
|---|---|---|
| Cheese sticks $3.50 | Roast Beef $3.95 | Lemonade $1.00 |
| Nachos $2.95 | Club $4.95 | Iced Tea $1.00 |
| Chicken wings $3.95 | Chicken $4.95 | Cola $1.00 |
| | Tuna $3.75 | Coffee $1.00 |

**EXAMPLE**

Sandra and Joyce went to lunch at The Stable. Sandra had a club sandwich and a lemonade. Joyce wanted a chicken sandwich but had only enough money for nachos and iced tea. About how much money did Joyce have to spend?

**Necessary information:** cost of nachos and iced tea

$2.95 + $1.00 = $3.95

1. Manny phoned in an order for a tuna sandwich and an order of cheese sticks. He was told it would cost an extra $1.00 to have it delivered, so he picked up his order. What was his bill?

   **Necessary information:** _____

2. Jean ordered chicken wings, a club sandwich, and a cola. Thomas ordered the same, except he also had coffee. How much did Thomas spend for lunch at The Stable?

   **Necessary information:** _____

3. Connie served a table of 10 whose bill came to $66.50, including 2 coffees to go. A tip of $10.00 was then added to the bill. How much money did she collect from the group?

   **Necessary information:** _____

**Check your answers on page 65.**

# SUBTRACTION SKILLS

## Whole Numbers and Money

Many real-life situations require you to compare or find differences between money amounts.

**Directions:** Compare the different amounts shown on the pay stub below by answering the following questions.

| Social Security No. | Name | | | | Pay Period | Pay Date |
|---|---|---|---|---|---|---|
| | Kerry Thomas | | | | Ending 3/27/9X | 3/31/9X |
| Earnings | | Type | Deduction | Type | Deduction | Type |
| 769 : 23 Reg | | | 18 : 50 Health | | | |

| This Pay | Gross Pay | Federal Income Tax | Soc. Sec. Tax | Medicare Tax | State Income Tax | Net Pay |
|---|---|---|---|---|---|---|
| | 769 : 23 | 115 : 38 | 47 : 69 | 11 : 15 | 23 : 08 | |
| YTD | 4,615 : 38 | 692 : 28 | 286 : 14 | 66 : 90 | 138 : 48 | 553.43 |

**EXAMPLE**

Find the difference between Kerry's gross pay and net pay for this pay period.

$$\begin{array}{r} \$769.23 \\ -553.43 \\ \hline \$215.80 \end{array}$$ (gross)
(net)
(difference)

1. How much more has Kerry paid year to date (YTD) in federal income tax than in state income tax?

2. By this time last year, Kerry had earned just $3,998.15 in gross pay. How much more has she earned by March 31 this year compared to last year?

3. A currency exchange charges Kerry a fee of $5.50 to cash her check. How much money does Kerry get back if she has the cashier take the fee out of her check?

4. Kerry puts $25.00 in a savings account each pay period. How much money does she have left of her net pay after cashing her check at the currency exchange and then making the savings deposit?

5. Kerry has both Medicare tax and health insurance payments deducted from her check. How much more does she pay for health insurance than for Medicare each pay period? (*Hint:* Find the Medicare Tax in the "This Pay" row.)

**Check your answers on page 66.**

# Deciding When to Add or Subtract

Choosing which operation to use can sometimes be difficult. After solving a problem, reread the question to make sure your answer makes sense.

**Directions:** For each problem, choose the expression that gives the correct answer. Then solve the expression and reread the question to see if your answer makes sense.

**EXAMPLE**

Gloria got a raise of $42.00 a week. If she was earning $280.00 a week before the raise, what does she earn now?

**(1)** $280.00 – $42.00

**(2)** $280.00 + $42.00

Gloria earns more now than before, so combining the numbers for a total of $322.00 makes sense.

1. On his diet, Mickey is allowed 950 total calories for breakfast and lunch and 1,050 calories for the rest of the day. How many calories is he allowed per day?

   **(1)** 1,050 – 950

   **(2)** 1,050 + 950

2. The average temperature in the Mariana Islands varies from 67° during winter to 88° during summer. What is the temperature range there?

   **(1)** 88° – 67°

   **(2)** 88° + 67°

3. Yvonne spent $75.68 on art supplies for one project, but then returned a sketch pad that cost $4.82. How much did she spend on the project?

   **(1)** $75.68 – $4.82

   **(2)** $75.68 + $4.82

4. The time in Chicago is 2 hours later than the time in Los Angeles. If a plane leaves Los Angeles at 8:00 P.M. headed for Chicago, what time was it in Chicago when the plane took off?

   **(1)** 8:00 P.M. – 2 hours

   **(2)** 8:00 P.M. + 2 hours

**Check your answers on page 66.**

# Addition and Subtraction: Information Needed

With practice, you'll find word problems easier to solve. You'll learn to quickly find necessary information and choose the correct operation.

**Directions:** Each set of problems is based on a story or situation. For each problem, circle the appropriate operation, list the information needed to solve the problem, and then find the answer. Check to make sure the answer makes sense. The first one has been started for you.

*Problems 1–3* refer to the advertisement at right.

**SPORTS COUPE**

$295 a month for 48 months

List Price $12,679
Cash rebate $555!

1. If you pay for this car on a 48-month loan, what would be the total cost of the January, February, and March payments?

   a. (Addition) or Subtraction
   b. Information needed:  $295 a month for 3 months
   c. Solution:

2. If you pay for this car on a 48-month loan, the total cost would be $14,160. How much less expensive is it to pay for the car all at once?

   a. Addition or Subtraction
   b. Information needed:
   c. Solution:

3. After one whole year of payments, how many payments would you have left to make on the loan listed in the advertisement?

   a. Addition or Subtraction
   b. Information needed:
   c. Solution:

*Problems 4–6* refer to the story below.

It is a 1,109-mile journey from Minneapolis to Yellowstone National Park. The trip takes about 20 hours by car. It is one hour earlier at Yellowstone National Park than in Minneapolis.

4. Jonathan and Ken traveled by car from Minneapolis to Yellowstone and then decided to drive another 367 miles to Glacier National Park. How many total miles did they drive to reach Glacier National Park?

   a. Addition or Subtraction
   b. Information needed:
   c. Solution:

5. The trip from Yellowstone to Glacier Park takes about 7 hours. How much longer does the trip take from Minneapolis to Yellowstone than the trip from Yellowstone to Glacier Park?

   **a.** Addition or Subtraction
   **b.** Information needed:
   **c.** Solution:

6. If Jonathan and Ken take the same route back to Minneapolis, how many hours should it take to get home from Glacier National Park?

   **a.** Addition or Subtraction
   **b.** Information needed:
   **c.** Solution:

*Problems 7–8* refer to the advertisement below.

| GRANT'S GROCERY | |
|---|---|
| Rolls (12 oz.) | 79¢ |
| Stuffing Cubes (8 oz.) | 79¢ |
| Sweet Gherkins (16 oz.) | Buy 1 at $2.59, get 1 FREE! |
| Applesauce (24 oz.) | 99¢ |
| Olives (5.75 oz.) | 89¢ |
| Cat Food (3.5 lb.) | $2.59 |
| Bathroom Tissue (4 pk./2 ply) | 99¢ |
| Cola (2 liters) | 99¢ |

7. Emily had a $.75 coupon for cat food. How much did the pet food cost?

   **a.** Addition or Subtraction
   **b.** Information needed:
   **c.** Solution:

8. Carole keeps a grocery list. So far this week, she has listed the following items: bathroom tissue, two packages of rolls, and applesauce. How much do the groceries on her list cost so far?

   **a.** Addition or Subtraction
   **b.** Information needed:
   **c.** Solution:

**Check your answers on page 66.**

# MULTIPLICATION SKILLS

Book 1
**Text Pages**
94–95

## Using Estimation in Word Problems

Estimation can make word problems easier to solve by:

• making numbers simpler and easier to use
• enabling you to quickly try different operations
• helping you check your answer to see if it is approximately correct

**Directions:** In each problem below, decide whether to add, subtract, or multiply. Then substitute round numbers to find an approximate answer (estimate). Finally, circle the exact answer using your estimate as a guide. Problem 1 has been started for you.

1. Alex pays $598.90 in rent each month. How much rent does he pay for a whole year?

   **Operation:** _multiply_

   **Substitute:** _$600_ for _$598.90_

   **Estimate:** _____

   **Exact Answer**
   (1) $3,490.70
   (2) $5,807.50
   (3) $7,186.80

2. The attendance for three nights of a high school play was as follows: 982 on Thursday, 998 on Friday, 1,010 on Saturday. What was the total attendance for the three nights?

   **Operation:** _____

   **Substitute:** _____ for _____

   and _____ for _____

   and _____ for _____

   **Estimate:** _____

   **Exact Answer**
   (1) 1,350
   (2) 2,990
   (3) 6,940

3. Melissa paid $50.25 for a coat that originally sold for $75.00. How much money did she save by buying the coat on sale?

   **Operation:** _____

   **Substitute:** _____ for _____

   **Estimate:** _____

   **Exact Answer**
   (1) $2.47
   (2) $24.75
   (3) $125.25

**Check your answers on page 67.**

# Solving Word Problems

In some situations, only an estimate is necessary. Other situations may require an exact answer.

**Directions:** For each problem, (a) decide whether an estimate or an exact answer is necessary, then (b) answer the question.

*The example and problems 1–3 refer to the items shown below.*

| Season's Greetings Clearance Sale | | |
|---|---|---|
| Sweaters | Reg. $49.99 | Now $25.99 |
| Ladies' Slacks | Reg. $35.99 | Now $16.99 |
| Ladies' Skirts | Reg. $44.99 | Now $25.49 |
| Men's Dress Shirts | Reg. $36.99 | Now $19.79 |
| Children's Boots | Reg. $24.99 | Now $15.75 |

**EXAMPLE**

Florence has a $50.00 gift certificate from Season's Greetings. If she buys a sweater and a skirt, will it cost more than her gift certificate?

a. Exact or (Estimate)

b. <u>Yes. A sweater costs about $26.00. A skirt costs about $25.00. Together they are more than $50.00.</u>

1. Ellen doesn't want to spend more than $60.00. If she buys her husband one dress shirt and her son a pair of boots, will she have enough to buy herself a pair of slacks, too?

   a. Exact or Estimate

   b. _____

2. Jean is going to write a check for her purchase. If she buys two sweaters and the tax is $3.12, how much should she write the check for?

   a. Exact or Estimate

   b. _____

   _____

3. How much is Jean saving by buying the two sweaters on sale?

   a. Exact or Estimate

   b. _____

   _____

**Check your answers on page 67.**

# DIVISION SKILLS

Book 1
**Text Pages**
113–115

## Division Word Problems

Division word problems often involve finding an average, an equal share, or the value of a single item. Sometimes the answer to a division problem is not a whole number; there is also a remainder. When checking your work, think how the remainder affects your final answer.

**Directions:** Work each problem below.

**EXAMPLE**

Wesley wants to tape a TV mini-series that is scheduled to last 5 hours (300 minutes). How many blank videotapes does he need if each tape lasts 120 minutes?

$$120\overline{)300} \quad \begin{array}{r} 2\,R\,60 \\ \underline{240} \\ 60 \end{array} \quad \text{or 3 blank tapes}$$

(He will need 3 blank tapes. He needs 2 plus 1 more for the remaining 60 minutes.)

1. A church group provides transportation for 23 of its members' children to attend summer camp. How many cars are needed to transport the children to camp if 5 children can fit in each car?

2. Hamburger buns are sold eight to a package. Leo is planning to make 30 hamburgers for the family picnic. How many packages of buns will he need?

3. Ruth wants to send out 68 cards for the holidays this year. If the cards she chooses come 12 to a box, how many boxes will she need?

4. Denise's car can travel 350 miles on a full tank of gas. If Denise must travel 750 miles, how many times will she need to fill the gas tank?

5. The Curtis family has $.50 gift certificates to a fast-food restaurant. How many will they need to redeem for a meal that totals $12.47?

6. Eileen is making cookies. She has 13 cups of flour. If each batch of cookies requires 2 cups of flour, how many full batches of cookies can she make?

**Check your answers on page 67.**

# Deciding When to Multiply or Divide

Sometimes you may have difficulty deciding whether to multiply or divide. Understanding the question will help. By checking to make sure the answer makes sense, you will know if you chose the correct operation.

**Directions:** For each of the following problems, choose the answer that makes the most sense.

*Problems 1– 4* are based on the classified advertisement below.

| **Rent/Apartments** |
| --- |
| MODERN SPACIOUS, PRIVATE 2nd floor. 6 miles from Manchester in PA. (1) bedroom, $384. (2) bedroom, $444. Both include stove, refrigerator, air conditioner, water and garbage. No pets. Call 717-555-8961. |

1. If Clarissa and Madeline decide to rent the two bedroom apartment and split the cost, how much will each pay per month for rent?

   **(1)** Multiplication: $888

   **(2)** Division: $222

2. John signs a lease to rent the one-bedroom apartment for a full year. How much will a year's rent cost him?

   **(1)** Multiplication: $4,608

   **(2)** Division: $32

3. John, who is renting the one-bedroom apartment, works in Manchester. Because he works six days a week, he makes the trip twelve times a week. How many miles does he drive to and from work each week?

   **(1)** Multiplication: 72 miles

   **(2)** Division: 2 miles

4. Mr. Willis, the apartment manager, placed the classified ad to run sixteen times for a total cost of $74.72. How much did it cost him each time it ran in the paper?

   **(1)** Multiplication: $1,195.52

   **(2)** Division: $4.67

**Check your answers on page 67.**

# Solving Word Problems

In real life, no one tells you if a problem is solved by adding, subtracting, multiplying, or dividing. Your first step in choosing an operation is to understand the question. Then identify the information that is needed.

**Directions:** List the information needed to answer each question. Then place an X in front of the necessary operation. (*Hint:* Use your estimation skills to be sure your answer choice makes sense.)

---

**EXAMPLE**

Katie received a coupon in the mail for a $5.00 discount on any purchase of $25.00 or more at a nearby clothing store.  If she purchases a skirt that is marked $32.99, how much will the skirt cost?

**Information needed:** $32.99 cost of skirt, $5.00 discount

**Operation:**   ___addition

X subtraction

___multiplication

___division

(*Hint:* If you round $32.99 to $33.00 and subtract $5.00, you get $28.00 as an approximate answer. This answer makes sense, so your choice seems correct.)

*Problems 1–3* are based on the chart below.

| County Hospital | | |
|---|---|---|
| **Time Period** | **Expected Loss** | **Actual Loss** |
| Mar., Apr., May, June | $400,000 | $440,000 |
| July, Aug., Sept., Oct. | $490,000 | $165,000 |

1. On the **average**, how much money did the hospital lose each month from July through October?

**Information needed:** _____

**Operation:**   ___addition

___subtraction

___multiplication

___division

**2.** How much more money did the hospital expect to lose from July through October than it actually lost?

**Information needed:** _____

**Operation:**   ____addition

                 ____subtraction

                 ____multiplication

                 ____division

**3.** How much money did the hospital lose altogether from March through October?

**Information needed:** _____

**Operation:**   ____addition

                 ____subtraction

                 ____multiplication

                 ____division

*Problems 4–5 are based on the following story.*

Lynn is buying cookies to send to her daughter's first-grade class for a Halloween party. There are 27 children in the class. Lynn decides to buy 11 boxes of cookies. Each box contains 12 cookies and costs $2.59.

**4.** How many cookies will she get from the 11 boxes?

**Information needed:** _____

**Operation:**   ____addition

                 ____subtraction

                 ____multiplication

                 ____division

**5.** How much will she pay for all the cookies?

**Information needed:** _____

**Operation:**   ____addition

                 ____subtraction

                 ____multiplication

                 ____division

**Check your answers on page 67.**

# Solving Word Problems—More Practice

In the previous lesson, you had to list information and identify the necessary operation. Now you will practice these same skills in a slightly different way.

**Directions:** In each problem below, identify the operation and estimate an answer. As always, check your answer to make sure it makes sense.

*Problems 1–5* are based on the following story.

The bowling standings listed in the local paper's sports section show that a team called the Stoppers has won 27 games and lost 18 so far. It has 15 games left to play. Its star player got scores of 119, 153, and 178 in her first 3 games this season.

1. How many games have the Stoppers played so far?

   **Operation:** _____

   **Estimate:** _____


2. By how much did the Stoppers' star player increase her score from her first game to her second?

   **Operation:** _____

   **Estimate:** _____


3. For the first 3 games, the team's worst player had a combined total score of 294. What is that player's average score for these games?

   **Operation:** _____

   **Estimate:** _____


4. The Stoppers' star player had a total of 2,430 pins for the last 12 games. What score did she average per game for these last games?

   **Operation:** _____

   **Estimate:** _____


5. If the Stoppers lost 12 of their last 15 games, how many games would they have lost altogether this year?

   **Operation:** _____

   **Estimate:** _____

*Problems 6–10* are based on the following story.

Anthony called a local newspaper to find the rates for placing an ad in the help wanted section. The rates were as follows:

> Sunday edition: $20.00 per line
> Weekly edition:
> 1 day:          $4.75 per line per day
> 2 days:        $4.25 per line per day
> 3 or more days: $3.75 per line per day
>
> A minimum of 3 lines is required.

**6.** What is the minimum amount Anthony would have to pay to run a help wanted ad in Sunday's paper?

**Operation:** _____

**Estimate:** _____

**7.** Anthony decides to run a 5-line ad in Saturday's paper. About how much will the ad cost?

**Operation:** _____

**Estimate:** _____

**8.** Anthony paid $100 to run the same ad in Sunday's paper. About how much more did it cost to run the ad in Sunday's paper than in Saturday's paper?

**Operation:** _____

**Estimate:** _____

**9.** To run a 5-line weekly ad for 3 days would cost $56.25. About how much does it cost to run the ad per day?

**Operation:** _____

**Estimate:** _____

**10.** Anthony ran 3 ads over the past 4 months. They cost $85, $56.25, and $38. About how much did the 3 ads cost altogether?

**Operation:** _____

**Estimate:** _____

**Check your answers on page 68.**

## Multi-Step Word Problems

A multi-step word problem requires two or more steps for a solution. When a multi-step problem is broken down into one-step problems, it becomes easier to solve.

**Directions:** In each of the following problems, write a solution sentence. Then break down the problem into one-step problems in steps 1 and 2. Use estimation to check your answers.

*The example and problems 1–5 are based on the following want ad.*

---

CONSTRUCTION

Carpenters to $22 per hour. Laborers to $16 per hour. Drywall to $14.75 per hour. Masons and tenders to $22.50 per hour. Call 1-800-555-2971.

---

**EXAMPLE**

Josh gets a job as a top-paid tender, and his wife Angela is a top-paid drywall person. How much are their combined earnings per 40-hour week?

**Solution sentence:** Total earnings = Josh's earnings + Angela's earnings

**Step 1:** 40 hr. X $22.50 = $900    40 hr. x $14.75 = $590

**(Multiply to find the earnings of each person.)**

**Step 2:** $900 + $590 = $1,490

**(Add the two total earnings together.)**

1. How much more does the top-paid carpenter make per 40-hour week at the company than the top-paid laborer?

**Solution sentence:** _____

_____

**Step 1:** _____

**Step 2:** _____

**2.** Kim is a top-paid mason. What is his take-home pay for an 80-hour pay period if a total of $695 is taken out in deductions?

**Solution sentence:** _____

_____

**Step 1:** _____

**Step 2:** _____

**3.** Lea is an apprentice carpenter. She earns $430 per 40-hour week before deductions. How much less per hour does she earn than the top-paid carpenter?

**Solution sentence:** _____

_____

**Step 1:** _____

**Step 2:** _____

**4.** Martin, a top-paid laborer, was fortunate enough to average 40 working hours a week for 50 weeks last year. How much did he earn for the year (before deductions)?

**Solution sentence:** _____

_____

**Step 1:** _____

**Step 2:** _____

**5.** January was a slow month. Carl, a top-paid mason, worked only 100 hours that month. If he usually works at least 160 hours a month, how much less did he earn in January?

**Solution sentence:** _____

_____

**Step 1:** _____

**Step 2:** _____

**Check your answers on page 68.**

# Estimation with Measurement

In the United States we use both standard (American) and metric measuring units for labeling length, weight, and liquid measures. Time units are the same in both systems.

**Directions:** Use estimation and circle the correct answer in each problem.

*The example and problems 1–2 are based on the following story.*

Janet has a punch recipe that calls for 2 quarts of ginger ale, 1 quart of lemon-lime soda, and 1 quart of sherbet.

**EXAMPLE**

The grocery store carries lemon-lime soda in metric sizes only. Which size bottle does Janet need?

**(1)** .5 liter    **(2)** 1 liter    **(3)** 2 liters

1. The store sells sherbet in varying size containers. Which size comes closest to what Janet needs?

   **(1)** 8 ounces    **(2)** 16 ounces    **(3)** 36 ounces

2. Which ingredient in Janet's recipe requires a half-gallon size?

   **(1)** ginger ale    **(2)** lemon-lime soda    **(3)** sherbet

*Problems 3–5 are based on the following story.*

In 1912, Jim Thorpe, a Native American, won the Olympic decathlon and in 1950 was voted the greatest athlete of the first half century. Among his 1912 achievements were: running the 1,500-meter race in 4 minutes, 40.1 seconds; throwing a javelin 45.70 meters; and jumping 6 feet, $1\frac{1}{2}$ inches in the high jump.

3. If 1 meter is slightly larger than 1 yard, about how many **feet** did Jim Thorpe throw the javelin?

   **(1)** 15 feet    **(2)** 45 feet    **(3)** 135 feet

4. Jim Thorpe's high jump measured just a little shorter than _____.

   **(1)** 1 meter    **(2)** 2 meters    **(3)** 3 meters

5. The 1912 decathlon entrant from Finland ran the 1,500-meter race in 273.9 seconds. How many minutes is this equal to?

   **(1)** 4 min., 33.9 sec.    **(2)** 9 min., 3.9 sec.    **(3)** 27 min., 39 sec.

**Check your answers on page 68.**

# Measurement Problems

Measurement word problems are unlike other types of math problems. Answers often must be **simplified** by converting from one unit to another.

**Directions:** Solve the following problems in the spaces provided. **Be sure to simplify your final answers.**

**EXAMPLE**

In trying to get together enough flour to bake bread, Alma found 1 cup, 2 ounces in a flour sack and 2 cups, 7 ounces in the canister. If she needs 4 cups of flour, does she have enough?

$$
\begin{array}{r}
1 \text{ c. } 2 oz. \\
+\ 2 \text{ c. } 7 oz. \\
\hline
3 \text{ c. } 9 oz.
\end{array}
$$
= 4c. 1oz. (9oz. = 1c. 1oz.) Yes, she has enough flour.

*Problems 1–2 are based on the following story.*

Real Fresh Fruit Drink comes in 1.5-liter bottles. One serving contains 250 milliliters.

1. How many servings are in one bottle of Real Fresh Fruit Drink?

2. If there are 120 calories in a half liter of Real Fresh Fruit Drink, how many calories are in one serving?

*Problems 3–4 are based on the following story.*

Noreen and Ed's baby boy weighed 8 pounds, 14 ounces at birth. By six months of age, he weighed 17 pounds, 8 ounces.

3. How much weight had the baby gained by six months of age?

4. Most doctors like the weight of a baby to double from birth to six months. Did the weight of Noreen and Ed's baby double?

*Problems 5–6 are based on the following story.*

On a 10-kilometer charity walkathon, the first rest stop is 2 kilometers, 300 meters away from the start.

5. How far from the finish line are the walkers when they reach the first rest stop?

6. The second rest stop is 2 kilometers, 700 meters from the first rest stop. How far along in the race are the walkers when they reach the second rest stop?

**Check your answers on page 69.**

# Perimeter, Area, and Volume

• Perimeter is the distance around an object.
• Area is the measure of the surface of an object.
• Volume is the measure of space taken up by an object.

Although these are three very different measurements, it is sometimes difficult to tell which one you are being asked to find in a word problem.

**Directions:** Identify what you are being asked to find by writing *perimeter, area,* or *volume* in the blank after each of the following problems. Then find the answer. (*Hint:* Draw a picture to help you see the problem.)

**EXAMPLE**

How much carpeting do the Carsons have to order for their living room that measures 4 yards by 6 yards?

**a.** This problem is asking me to find ___*area*___.

**b.** Answer: ___4 yd. × 6 yd. = 24 sq. yd.___

4 yd.

6 yd.

*Problems 1–3 are based on the following story.*

A room, 9 feet wide by 11 feet long, is being redecorated. A wallpaper trim is being hung around the entire top of the room. One wall, 9 feet wide and 8 feet high, is being wallpapered.

1. How many feet of trim are needed?

   **a.** This problem is asking me to find _____.

   **b.** Answer: _____

2. How much wallpaper is needed for the one wall?

   **a.** This problem is asking me to find _____.

   **b.** Answer: _____

3. There is a hole in one wall that needs to be filled. The hole is 3 inches across, 2 inches high, and 1 inch deep. How many cubic inches of filler are needed?

   **a.** This problem is asking me to find _____.

   **b.** Answer: _____

**Check your answers on page 69.**

# Squares, Cubes, and Square Roots

- The square of a number is that number multiplied by itself.
- The cube of a number is that number multiplied by itself twice.
- The square root of a number is found by asking, "What number times itself equals this number?"

**Directions:** Fill in the missing values. When done correctly, each challenge will start and end with the same number. The first one is done for you.

**Challenge 1:** Start with the number 2.

**a.** Cube the given number ($2^3$). ____8____ (*Hint:* $2 \times 2 \times 2 = 8$)

**b.** Add 2 to answer $a$ and square the sum. _____ [*Hint:* $(8 + 2)^2 = 100$]

**c.** Find the square root of answer $b$. _____ (*Hint:* $\sqrt{100}$)

**d.** Subtract 2 from answer $c$ and square the difference.

**e.** Divide answer $d$ by 2 and add 4. _____

**f.** Find the square root of answer $e$. _____

**g.** Divide answer $f$ by 3. (*Hint:* You should end up with the number you were given at the beginning of the challenge.)

**Challenge 2:** Start with the number 9.

**a.** Find the square root of the given number. _____

**b.** Cube answer $a$. _____

**c.** Add 3 to answer $b$ and square the sum. _____

**d.** Divide answer $c$ by 9. _____

**e.** Find the square root of answer $d$ and subtract 1. _____

**Challenge 3:** Start with the number 13.

**a.** Double the given number and subtract 1. _____

**b.** Find the square root of answer $a$. _____

**c.** Cube answer $b$ and subtract 4. _____

**d.** Find the square root of answer $c$ and add 1. _____

**e.** Square answer $d$. _____

**f.** Add 5 squared to answer $e$. _____

**g.** Find the square root of answer $f$. _____

**Check your answers on page 69.**

# BREAKTHROUGHS IN MATH

## Book 2

# SKILLS REVIEW

## Steps in Solving Word Problems

Most math problems found in everyday life are word problems. Therefore, it is very important to develop word problem skills.

**Directions:** For each step, circle the correct information from the choices given in parentheses. Some steps may require more than one answer. Step 1 is done as an example.

*Steps 1–5* refer to the chart and question below.

|  | **Film Developing** | |
|---|---|---|
|  | **One-Day Guarantee** | **Two-Day Guarantee** |
| 12-exposure | $1.99 | $1.59 |
| 24-exposure | 2.99 | 2.59 |
| 36-exposure | 3.99 | 3.59 |

CeCe had a coupon for $.75 off the cost of developing a roll of 24-exposure film. How much did it cost her to have a roll of 24 pictures developed in two days?

**Step 1.** **Understand** the question.

The question asks me to find the cost of developing (24-exposure film in 2 days, 24-exposure film in 1 day, 12-exposure film in 2 days).

**Step 2.** Find the **necessary information**.

I need the following information to solve the problem: ($.75 coupon, $2.99 for developing, $2.59 for developing).

**Step 3.** Choose an arithmetic **operation**.

The operation I need to use to solve this problem is (addition, subtraction, multiplication, division).

**Step 4.** **Solve** the problem.

The answer is ($3.34, $2.59, $1.84).

**Step 5.** **Check** to see if the answer makes sense.

*Think*: My answer should be (less than, more than) the original price of $2.59.

**Check your answers on page 69.**

# Using Estimates to Check Answers

The final step in solving a word problem is to check your answer. If your math is correct and your answer makes sense, you can feel confident you have the right answer. Estimation can help you complete this last step.

**Directions:** For each problem: (a) circle the operation needed to find the answer; (b) estimate an answer; (c) compare your estimate and the exact answer given; and (d) if the exact answer seems incorrect, solve the problem to find the exact answer. Problem 1 has been started for you.

*Problems 1–3* are based on the following story.

Last year, Marian Barber earned $16,398. Her husband, Ernie, was paid $23,740 for the year. This year, Marian figures she will earn $18,125, but Ernie will receive a raise of just $1,020.

1. What was the combined income of the Barbers last year?

   **a.** Operation: (Add) Subtract Multiply Divide

   **b.** Estimate: *$16,000 + $24,000 = $40,000*

   **c.** Exact answer: $18,772

   Does the exact answer seem correct? Yes No

   **d.** Solution: _____

2. How much was Ernie paid per month last year?

   **a.** Operation: Add Subtract Multiply Divide

   **b.** Estimate: _____

   **c.** Exact answer: $197.83

   Does the exact answer seem correct? Yes No

   **d.** Solution: _____

3. How much was Marian's raise this year?

   **a.** Operation: Add Subtract Multiply Divide

   **b.** Estimate: _____

   **c.** Exact answer: $1,727

   Does the exact answer seem correct? Yes No

   **d.** Solution: _____

**Check your answers on page 69.**

# Expressions and Order of Operations

An arithmetic expression is often used to show the computation steps of a multi-step word problem. Once the expression has been written, it must be solved in a specific order of operations:

**Step 1.** Do the arithmetic indicated within parentheses first.
**Step 2.** Starting at the left, do all multiplication and division.
**Step 3.** Starting at the left, do all addition and subtraction, adding or subtracting two numbers at a time.

**Directions:** For each problem, circle the correct expression. Then solve each problem by following the order of operations.

*Problems 1–3* refer to the chart below and involve weekday telephone rates. Telephone charges are based on a point system for each call made.

| **Dial Direct: Weekday Point System** | | |
|---|---|---|
| **Distance in Miles** | **Points Charged First Minute** | **Each Additional Minute** |
| 1–25 | 25 | 10 |
| 26–50 | 45 | 28 |
| 51–75 | 55 | 34 |
| 76–100 | 60 | 37 |
| over 100 | 75 | 40 |
| Extra points charged: 150 for other operator-assisted calls | | |

1. Joan and Marie live 55 miles apart. How many points will be charged for a direct-dial 16-minute phone call between them?

   **(1)** $55 \times 16$          **Solution**

   **(2)** $55 + (15 \times 34)$

   **(3)** $55 + 16 \times 34$

2. Marcia and Kirby live 860 miles apart. How many points will be charged for a 25-minute direct-dial phone call between them?

   **(1)** $75 \times 25$          **Solution**

   **(2)** $75 + (24 \times 40)$

   **(3)** $75 \times 25 + 34$

3. Greg made a 37-minute operator-assisted call to his girlfriend 10 miles away at work. How many points were charged for the call?

   **(1)** $25 \times 37 + 150$          **Solution**

   **(2)** $25 + (36 \times 10)$

   **(3)** $25 + (36 \times 10) + 150$

**Check your answers on page 70.**

# DECIMALS, FRACTIONS, AND PERCENTS

Book 2
**Text Pages**
30–33

## Numbers Smaller than 1

There are three ways to mathematically write numbers that are smaller than one: decimal fractions, common fractions, and percents. Each is used for specific purposes. For example, decimals are used in our money system, fractions in recipes, and percents in interest rates.

**Directions:** Match each occupation with a sample of how a person in that job would use a number smaller than one. The first problem is done as an example.

1. __7__ a. bank clerk                    (1) 10% mortgage rate

   ____ b. cook                           (2) ¾-inch nails

   ____ c. grocery clerk                  (3) .005 ml of medicine

   ____ d. carpenter                      (4) 8% unemployment

   ____ e. clothing manager              (5) ⅞ yard of fabric

   ____ f. newsstand salesperson         (6) $.52 for a candy bar

   ____ g. loan officer                  (7̸) 5% interest on savings

   ____ h. seamstress                    (8) ½ cup chopped onions

   ____ i. doctor                        (9) 50% off coats storewide

   ____ j. economist                     (10) $.35 for a newspaper

Now change each of the following to an equivalent as indicated.

**EXAMPLE**

10% mortgage rate means __$ .10__ interest is paid on every dollar borrowed.

2. .005 ml of medicine means $\frac{\square}{1,000}$ ml dosage.

3. 8% unemployment means $\frac{\square}{100}$ workers are unemployed.

4. $.52 for a candy bar means $\frac{52}{\square}$ of a dollar.

5. 5% interest on savings means _____ is added to each $1.00 saved.

6. 50% off coats means the original cost is reduced by _____ per dollar.

**Check your answers on page 70.**

# DECIMAL SKILLS

## Comparing and Ordering Decimal Fractions

Decimal fractions can be compared and ordered easily when they have the same number of decimal places.

**Directions:** Compare the values of the decimal fractions in each group, then put them in order from **smallest to largest**.

**EXAMPLE**

Quantity of sodium in different candy bars:

.5 grams          .005 grams          .05 grams          .55 grams

.005 grams , .050 grams , .500 grams , .550 grams

(*Note:* Zeros were added to the end of some decimals to give them the same number of places.)

1. Batting averages of four baseball players:

   .198          .270          .209          .189

2. Amount of tax on a dollar in various states:

   $.065          $.05          $.0525          $.06

3. Amount of perfume in different sizes of sample bottles:

   .75 ounces          .5 ounces          .25 ounces          .098 ounces

4. Lengths of various micrometer readings:

   .12 mm          .061 mm          .0538 mm          .1175 mm

5. Total points attained by Olympic athletes in Nordic skiing:

   398.9          398.39          398.780          398.825

6. Cost of a gallon of gas at different gas stations:

   $1.498          $1.30          $1.379          $1.289

**Check your answers on page 70.**

# Rounding Decimal Fractions

Sometimes money amounts are given in decimal parts of cents—more than two numbers following the decimal point. To find actual unit costs, you round these amounts to the nearest cent.

**Directions:** Grocery stores usually list the unit prices of items along with the prices of the items themselves. Gasoline stations list their prices per gallon. For each of the following unit prices, round to the nearest cent. Then circle the least expensive item in each group.

**EXAMPLE**

$.4475 per pint for Silly Soda = _$ .45_ per pint.

$.4395 per pint for Bubble Soda = _$ .44_ per pint.

$.4349 per pint for (generic soda) = _$ .43_ per pint.

1. $.07156 per ounce for Whitcomb's Mayonnaise = _____ per ounce.

   $.0698 per ounce for Season's Mayonnaise = _____ per ounce.

   $.06099 per ounce for Jane Newman's Mayonnaise = _____ per ounce.

2. $.929 per quart of Regent's milk = _____ per quart.

   $.844 per quart of Purity milk = _____ per quart.

   $.9350 per quart of Health-Tech milk = _____ per quart.

3. $.765 per square foot of Hall's Gift Wrap = _____ per sq. ft.

   $.778 per square foot of Precious Gift Wrap = _____ per sq. ft.

   $.7803 per square foot of Glory Gift Wrap = _____ per sq. ft.

4. $.28416 per ounce of Tasty Treat Cereal = _____ per ounce.

   $.289 per ounce of Crunchy Crisp Cereal = _____ per ounce.

   $.2912 per ounce of Sudden Surprise Cereal = _____ per ounce.

5. $1.379 per gallon of gas = _____ per gallon.

   $1.399 per gallon of gas = _____ per gallon.

   $1.311 per gallon of gas = _____ per gallon.

**Check your answers on page 70.**

# Solving Math Word Problems

The more practice you get doing word problems, the more skilled you become.

**Directions:** In the following problems, circle the arithmetic expressions that give the correct answer.

---

**EXAMPLE**

---

Dan Dritchard's earned run average (ERA) was 2.83 his first year in professional baseball. He lowered his ERA by .35 the following year. What was his ERA for the second year?

**(1)** 2.83 + .35

**(2)** 2.83 − .35  (showing a decrease in his ERA)

**(3)** 2.83 × .35

**(4)** 2.83 ÷ .35

1. Dan had hoped to achieve a 2.50 ERA his first year in professional baseball. By how much did he miss his goal?

   **(1)** 2.83 − 2.50

   **(2)** 2.50 − 2.83

   **(3)** 2.50 + 2.83

   **(4)** 2.50 ÷ 2.83

2. Dan's ERA for his last two seasons was 3.03 and 2.97. What was his average ERA for those two seasons?

   **(1)** (3.03 + 2.97) ÷ 2

   **(2)** 3.03 + 2.97 ÷ 2

   **(3)** (3.03 + 2.97) × 2

   **(4)** 3.03 + 2.97 × 2

*Use the drawing below to answer problems 3–4.*

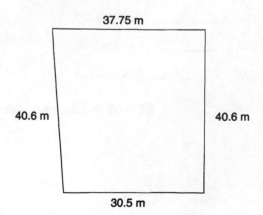

37.75 m

40.6 m          40.6 m

30.5 m

**3.** Derrick is planning to have a fence put around the property shown on page 34. How many meters of fencing does he need?

(1) 37.75 + 40.6 + 30.5 + 40.6

(2) 37.75 + 40.6

(3) 37.75 × 40.6

(4) 37.75 + 40.6 − 30.5 − 40.6

**4.** How much will Derrick pay for the installation of the fence if the workmen charge him $10.80 per hour and it takes them 7.25 hours to install it?

(1) $10.80 + 7.25

(2) $10.80 − 7.25

(3) $10.80 × 7.25

(4) $10.80 ÷ 7.25

*Use the drawing below to answer problems 5–6.*

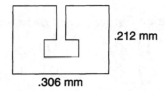

.212 mm

.306 mm

**5.** A machinist was making a tool part that needed a gap of exactly .07 millimeters (mm). After cutting the part and measuring the gap, the machinist found he had a gap of .058 mm. How much more did he need to cut away?

(1) .07 + .058

(2) .07 − .058

(3) .07 × .058

(4) .07 ÷ .058

**6.** The machinist must also make a metal plate to fit exactly over the surface of the part as shown, including the gap. What will be the surface area of the plate?

(1) .212 + .306

(2) .306 − .212

(3) .212 × .306

(4) .306 ÷ .212

**Check your answers on page 70.**

# Solving Multi-Step Word Problems

**Directions:** All solutions involve more than one step or operation. For each problem, fill in the missing information.

*The example and problems 1–3 are based on the following price list.*

| Service | Priority Next Day Morning | Overnight Next Day Afternoon | 2nd Day Morning | Overnight Letter |
|---------|---------------------------|------------------------------|-----------------|------------------|
|         | 5 lb./10 lb. | 5 lb./10 lb. | 5 lb./10 lb. | |
| Choice Parcel | $30.87/$43.94 | $17.50/n/a | $13.50/$18.50 | $13.00 |
| American Package | 18.50/ 26.00 | n/a/n/a | 7.75/ 13.00 | 9.75 |
| U.S. Post Office | | | | 9.95 |

*Note:* Packages weighing up to 5 lb. are charged the 5-lb. rate. Packages weighing between 5 lb. and 10 lb. are charged the 10-lb. rate.

n/a: not available

**EXAMPLE**

A 4.75-pound box of books needs to go out Priority Next Day Morning and a 6-pound box of fliers needs to be sent Second Day Morning. How much more would it cost to send the packages Choice Parcel than American Package Service?

**Difference in cost = cost of Choice Parcel – cost of American Package**

$$= \quad (30.87 + 18.50) \quad - \quad (18.50 + 13.00)$$

$$= \underline{\quad 49.37 \quad} - \underline{\quad 31.50 \quad}$$

**Difference in cost =** $\underline{\quad \$17.87 \quad}$

1. How much less would it cost to send two overnight letters through American Package Service than through the post office?

   **Total savings = difference in overnight letter cost x 2 letters**

   $$= \quad ( \underline{\hspace{4cm}} ) \times 2$$

   **Total savings =** $\underline{\hspace{4cm}}$

2. How much money would it cost to send four 9-pound packages by American Package Second Day Morning and two 3.6-pound packages by Choice Next Day Afternoon delivery?

   **Total charges = cost of American Package delivery +** $\underline{\hspace{5cm}}$

   $$= (13.00 \times 4) + (17.50 \times 2)$$

   **Total charges =** $\underline{\hspace{4cm}}$

**3.** How much more does it cost per pound to send a 10-pound package by Priority Next Day Morning through Choice Parcel than through American Package?

**Difference in cost per lb. = Choice's cost per lb. – American's cost per lb.**

$$= (43.94 \div 10) - (\underline{\hspace{3cm}})$$

**Difference in cost per lb. =** _____

*Problems 4–6* are based on the following label.

**Complete Vitamin Tablet**
**Directions:** Take one a day with the meal of your choice. Each tablet contains:

| Vitamins | Quantity |
|---|---|
| Vitamin A | 5,000 IU |
| Vitamin D | 400 IU |
| Vitamin E | 30 IU |
| Vitamin C | 00 mg |
| Vitamin B1 | 1.5 mg |
| Vitamin B2 | 1.7 mg |
| Niacin | 20 mg |
| Vitamin B6 | 2 mg |

**4.** Jack took two Complete Vitamin Tablets and a liquid vitamin C supplement of 49.75 mg. How much vitamin C did he take in all?

**Amount of vitamin C = amount in 2 vitamin tablets + amount in liquid**

$$= (\underline{\hspace{3cm}}) + 49.75 \text{ mg}$$

**Amount of vitamin C =** _____

**5.** Les took one Complete Vitamin Tablet. Then he ate a bowl of cereal with milk that contained 5 mg of niacin and a piece of toast with margarine that contained .45 mg of niacin. How much niacin did Les consume at breakfast?

**Amount of niacin = amount in food + amount in vitamin**

$$= (5 \text{ mg} + .45 \text{ mg}) + \underline{\hspace{3cm}}$$

**Amount of niacin =** _____

**6.** Maggie takes a Stress Caplet that contains a vitamin B complex totaling 31.2 mg. How much more of the vitamin Bs does she get in the Stress Caplet than she would get in a Complete Vitamin Tablet? (*Note:* Niacin counts as a B vitamin.)

**Difference in vitamin B amounts = amount in Stress Caplet –** _____

$$= 31.2 \text{ mg} - (1.5 \text{ mg} + 1.7 \text{ mg} + 20 \text{ mg} + 2 \text{ mg})$$

**Difference in vitamin B amounts =** _____

Check your answers on page 70.

# COMMON FRACTION SKILLS

Book 2
**Text Page**
71

## Comparing Common Fractions

Sometimes you need to know which of several fractions is smallest or largest. In order to compare fractions, write them with the same denominator.

**Directions:** To solve the problems below, write each group of fractions with a common denominator. Then answer the question. Problem 1 has been started for you.

1. Jim was doing some home repair and bought $\frac{3}{16}$-inch nails. The hardware store also sells the following sizes of nails.

   $\frac{3}{4}$ inch     = $\frac{12}{16}$ _____

   $\frac{7}{16}$ inch    = _____

   $\frac{1}{2}$ inch     = _____

   $\frac{3}{8}$ inch     = _____

   Jim now needs nails twice as big as the last ones he bought. What size nail does he need? _____

2. A carpenter wants to cut the following lengths from oversized boards:

   $\frac{9}{16}$ inch = _____

   $\frac{7}{8}$ inch = _____

   $\frac{1}{4}$ inch = _____

   $\frac{5}{32}$ inch = _____

   Which was closest to a half-inch cut? _____

   Which was the smallest cut? _____

3. A newspaper article said that $\frac{1}{8}$ of our tax dollars in one year went toward the education of our country's youth.

   Defense $\frac{5}{16}$ = _____

   Health/Welfare $\frac{1}{4}$ = _____

   Transportation $\frac{3}{16}$ = _____

   Other $\frac{1}{8}$ = _____

   Which of the expenses is **more than double** that amount? _____

**Check your answers on page 70.**

# Finding What Fraction a Part Is of a Whole

A fraction describes a part of a whole. For example, $\frac{5}{12}$ could describe part of a whole year (5 months out of 12 months).

**Directions:** Express each amount as a part of a whole. Write each fraction in its most reduced form.

One year has 52 weeks. What part of 52 is

. . . 2 weeks' vacation? $\frac{2}{52} = \frac{1}{26}$

1. . . . a 13-week term? _____

2. . . . a 28-week layoff? _____

Ron makes $2,000 a month. What part of $2,000 is

3. . . . rent of $600? _____

4. . . . utilities of $200? _____

5. . . . car payment of $250? _____

6. . . . food bills of $400? _____

1,760 yards are in one mile. What part of 1,760 is

7. . . . a 50-yard dash? _____

8. . . . a 100-yard dash? _____

9. . . . an 880-yard relay race? _____

Diane has one quart (32 ounces) of milk. She uses parts of the quart at dinner. What part of 32 ounces is one

10. . . . cup (8 ounces) used in the mashed potatoes? _____

11. . . . pint (16 ounces) used in a pitcher for coffee? _____

12. . . . 6-ounce serving used in the baby's bottle? _____

**Check your answers on page 70.**

# Solving Fraction Word Problems

To some people, fraction word problems seem more difficult than other word problems. Substituting whole numbers for fractions can make these problems easier to set up. When checking your answer to see if it makes sense, keep the following in mind:

• When you **multiply** a number by a fraction smaller than one, your answer is a **smaller** number than the one you started with.

• When you **divide** a number by a fraction smaller than one, your answer is a **larger** number than the one you started with.

**Directions:** (1) Circle the fraction in each problem. (2) Write an arithmetic equation for each problem using whole numbers as substitutes. (3) Solve each problem using fractions and check to be sure the answer makes sense.

*Use the map below to do the example and problems 1–5.*

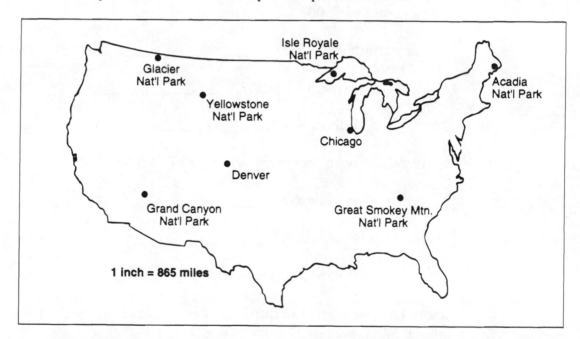

1 inch = 865 miles

---

**EXAMPLE**

How many miles is it from Glacier National Park to Yellowstone National Park if the distance on the map is $\frac{5}{8}$ inch and each inch equals 865 miles?

**Whole number equation:** $\underline{1 \times 865 = 865 \text{ miles (substituting 1 for } \frac{5}{8})}$

**Solution:** $\underline{\frac{5}{8} \times \frac{865}{1} = \frac{4,325}{8} = 540\frac{5}{8} \text{ miles}}$

(Does this answer make sense? Yes, because your answer should be smaller than the original number. If you had divided 865 miles by $\frac{5}{8}$ inch, you would have gotten 1,384 miles. A distance less than one inch cannot be greater than 865 miles.)

1. Trish wants to take her children camping at Isle Royale National Park, which is shown on the map to be $\frac{9}{16}$ inch from her home in Chicago. They will drive and then take a boat to the Island. What is the total distance between Chicago and Isle Royale National Park?

   **Whole number equation:** _____

   **Solution:** _____

2. It is $1\frac{3}{4}$ inches on the map from where Trish and her children live in Chicago to the entrance of Acadia National Park, Trish's second choice for a vacation. How many more inches on the map is Acadia National Park than Isle Royale National Park from Chicago?

   **Whole number equation:** _____

   **Solution:** _____

3. Instead of going straight to Glacier National Park, Joe takes a side trip from his home in Denver to meet some friends at the Grand Canyon. On the map, the Grand Canyon is $\frac{13}{16}$ inch from Denver, and Glacier National Park is $1\frac{3}{8}$ inches away from the Grand Canyon. How many inches does Joe need to multiply by 865 to find his total mileage for the trip?

   **Whole number equation:** _____

   **Solution:** _____

4. How many miles will Joe travel to get to Glacier National Park?

   **Whole number equation:** _____

   **Solution:** _____

5. The distance on the map from Glacier National Park to Yellowstone National Park is $\frac{5}{8}$ inch. The distance on the map from Glacier National Park to Acadia National Park is $3\frac{1}{2}$ inches. What is the difference in distance from Glacier National Park to Acadia National Park than from Glacier National Park to Yellowstone National Park?

   **Whole number equation:** _____

   **Solution:** _____

**Check your answers on page 71.**

# Comparison Word Problems

When you are given information in both fraction and decimal form and asked to compare them, rewrite each fraction as a decimal. Then compare the decimals.

**Directions:** In each problem, rewrite each fraction as a decimal. Then answer each question.

**EXAMPLE**

During one week, these employees recorded their hours of overtime as follows:

Bill       $8\frac{3}{4}$ hours   _8.75_

Chris      $8\frac{1}{4}$ hours   _8.25_

Beverly   8.5 hours   _8.5_

Which employee earned the most overtime that week? _Bill_ (8.75 is larger than both 8.25 and 8.5.)

1. Tom has the following nail sizes in his workroom:

   $2\frac{1}{2}$-inch _____

   2.75-inch _____

   $2\frac{3}{8}$-inch _____

   $2\frac{7}{16}$-inch _____

   Tom needs the smallest nail to use on a thin piece of wood. Which nail size will he use? _____

2. Sherri checks with four different banks in the area and is quoted the following interest rates on savings accounts:

   $4\frac{1}{4}$% _____

   4.20% _____

   $4\frac{1}{7}$% _____

   4.125% _____

   Which bank offers the best rate? _____

3. Mary is comparing three recipes for chicken soup. Each recipe requires different amounts of chicken:

   Recipe A  24 ounces of chicken _____

   Recipe B  2.25 pounds of chicken _____

   Recipe C  $2\frac{3}{8}$ pounds of chicken _____

   Which recipe uses the least amount of chicken? _____

4. Jake needs to drill a hole for a screw with a diameter of .125 inch. His drill bits are labeled $\frac{1}{8}$-inch and $\frac{3}{64}$-inch. Which drill bit should he use?

   _____

5. At the deli counter, Vicki asks for the following items:

   $1\frac{1}{2}$ pounds of sliced turkey _____

   $\frac{3}{4}$ pound of coleslaw _____

   16 ounces of macaroni salad _____

   The clerk gives her 1.49 pounds of turkey, .75 pound of coleslaw, and 1.15 pounds of macaroni salad. Were any of the amounts exactly what Vicki asked for? _____

   If so, which one(s)? _____

*Problems 6–7 are based on the following story.*

Greg ran in a 1,500-meter race on Monday, a 1.5-kilometer race on Friday, and a $1\frac{1}{2}$-kilometer race on Saturday.

6. Which of the three races was the longest? _____

7. A kilometer is equal to .62 mile. Which of the following distances most closely equals the distance that Greg ran in his first race?

   _____

   $\frac{9}{10}$ mile _____

   .87 mile _____

   .93 mile _____

**Check your answers on page 71.**

# Decimal and Fraction Multi-Step Word Problems

Many word problems contain both fractions and decimals. Many of these problems require more than one step to solve.

**Directions:** *For problems 1–3,* complete the solution sentence started for you, then solve the problem.

*All examples and problems on pages 44–45 are based on the following chart.*

**Overtime Hours**

Department: Quality Control

| Employee | Mon. | Tues. | Wed. | Thurs. | Fri. |
|---|---|---|---|---|---|
| Adell, S. | $\frac{1}{2}$ | $\frac{1}{4}$ | $\frac{3}{4}$ | $\frac{1}{2}$ | $\frac{1}{4}$ |
| Bass, T. | $\frac{1}{2}$ | $\frac{1}{2}$ | $1\frac{1}{2}$ | $1\frac{1}{4}$ | 0 |
| Brenner, E. | $\frac{3}{4}$ | $1\frac{1}{4}$ | $2\frac{1}{4}$ | 0 | 0 |
| Case, J. | 1 | $1\frac{1}{4}$ | $1\frac{1}{2}$ | 2 | $\frac{1}{2}$ |
| Dodd, M. | 0 | $\frac{1}{2}$ | 2 | $1\frac{3}{4}$ | $\frac{1}{4}$ |
| Freeman, I. | $1\frac{1}{2}$ | $\frac{3}{4}$ | $2\frac{1}{4}$ | 0 | 0 |

**EXAMPLE**

At the rate of $9.10 per hour for overtime work, how much did Ms. Freeman earn in overtime during the week shown in the chart?

**Overtime earnings = Number of overtime hours x Wages per overtime hour**

$$= (\underline{1\tfrac{1}{2} + \tfrac{3}{4} + 2\tfrac{1}{4}\quad}) \times \underline{\$9.10\quad}$$

$$= \underline{4\tfrac{1}{2}\quad} \times \underline{\$9.10\quad}$$

$$= \underline{4.5\quad} \times \underline{\$9.10\quad}$$

**Overtime earnings = $\underline{\$40.95\quad}$**

1. John Case worked $6\frac{1}{4}$ hours overtime that week. How many fewer hours of overtime did Ed Brenner work that week than John Case?

   **Difference in overtime hours = John Case's hours – _____**

   **= _____ – _____**

   **Difference in overtime hours = _____**

2. Mike Dodd earned a total of $31.50 in overtime that week. How much did he earn per hour in overtime?

   **Overtime earnings per hour = Total overtime earnings \_\_\_\_\_ Number of hours**
   **operation**
   **symbol**

   **= _____**

   **Overtime earnings per hour = _____**

**3.** Sue Adell had exactly the same number of overtime hours each week for all four weeks that month. How much overtime did she put in that month?

Total overtime hours = _____ x Number of weeks

= _____

Total overtime hours = _____

**Directions:** *For problems 4–5,* circle the number of the arithmetic expression that will give the correct answer to each question. **Do not solve the problems.**

EXAMPLE

Tim Bass normally earns $6.50 per hour. He gets $1\frac{1}{2}$ times that wage for overtime work. How much did he earn in overtime that week?

**(1)** $(\$6.50 \times 1\frac{1}{2}) \times (\frac{1}{2} + \frac{1}{2} + 1\frac{1}{2} + 1\frac{1}{4})$

**(2)** $(\$6.50 \times 1\frac{1}{2}) + (\frac{1}{2} + \frac{1}{2} + 1\frac{1}{2} + 1\frac{1}{4})$

**(3)** $(\$6.50 + 1\frac{1}{2}) \times (\frac{1}{2} + \frac{1}{2} + 1\frac{1}{2} + 1\frac{1}{4})$

**4.** How many more hours of overtime did the Quality Control employees work on Wednesday than Thursday?

**(1)** $(\frac{3}{4} + 1\frac{1}{2} + 2\frac{1}{4} + 1\frac{1}{2} + 2 + 2\frac{1}{4}) - (\frac{1}{2} - 1\frac{1}{4} - 2 - 1\frac{3}{4})$

**(2)** $(\frac{3}{4} + 1\frac{1}{2} + 2\frac{1}{4} + 1\frac{1}{2} + 2 + 2\frac{1}{4}) + (\frac{1}{2} - 1\frac{1}{4} - 2 - 1\frac{3}{4})$

**(3)** $(\frac{3}{4} + 1\frac{1}{2} + 2\frac{1}{4} + 1\frac{1}{2} + 2 + 2\frac{1}{4}) - (\frac{1}{2} + 1\frac{1}{4} + 2 + 1\frac{3}{4})$

**5.** Sue Adell earns $5.75 per hour for her regular 40-hour week and $8.63 per hour for overtime work. How much did Sue earn in total for the week shown?

**(1)** $(\$5.75 \times 40) + \$8.63 \times (\frac{1}{2} + \frac{1}{4} + \frac{3}{4} + \frac{1}{2} + \frac{1}{4})$

**(2)** $(\$5.75 + \$8.63) \times (\frac{1}{2} + \frac{1}{4} + \frac{3}{4} + \frac{1}{2} + \frac{1}{4}) + 40$

**(3)** $(\$5.75 \times 40) \times \$8.63 \times (\frac{1}{2} + \frac{1}{4} + \frac{3}{4} + \frac{1}{2} + \frac{1}{4})$

**Check your answers on page 71.**

# PERCENT SKILLS

## Word Problems: Percents, Decimals, and Fractions

Percents, decimals, and fractions all relate parts to a whole. You can change each form into another of the forms, but each has its special uses.

- **Decimals** are used in our money system and in metric measurement.
- **Fractions** are the basis of the English measuring system.
- **Percents** are used in banking, taxes, discounts, and interest rates.

**Directions:** Complete each of the following statements about part to whole relationships. The first one is done for you as an example.

*All problems on pages 46–47 are based on the following guide.*

---

**Family Motors Buyers' Guide**

**FM Sport**
**Standard:**

1.6-liter engine
5-speed manual
  transmission
Rack and pinion steering
Front disc brakes
AM-FM radio
$96\frac{1}{2}$-inch wheelbase

$164\frac{7}{10}$-inch overall length
$66\frac{4}{5}$-inch overall width
$11\frac{1}{4}$-cubic-foot luggage
  space
12-gallon fuel tank
Color choices: red, blue,
  silver, white, black
3-year/36,000-mile
  warranty

**Also available:**
Power steering
3-speed automatic
  transmission
9.9% financing
Hatchback with
  20-cubic-foot luggage
  space (with seat down)

**PRICE:** $10,999.99

---

**EXAMPLE**

There is a warning light that goes on when the FM Sport's gas tank has only 3 gallons left. At that point, it has used up ____$\frac{3}{4}$____ of the gas. (9 out of 12 or $\frac{9}{12}$ has been used; $\frac{9}{12} = \frac{3}{4}$.)   **fraction**

1. Joan is trying to decide which color car to get. She sees a magazine article that says 3 out of every 10 car buyers prefer red cars. She knows that "3 out of 10" is _____ or _____, of all car buyers.
   **fraction**        **percent**

2. Amanda's bank says it can give her an interest rate of $6\frac{3}{4}$% on a car loan. To compare that to Family Motors' interest rate, she changes $6\frac{3}{4}$% to 6._____%. Then she compares what that means in dollars.

   **decimal**

   6.9% means for every $100 of her loan she will pay _____ interest.

   **decimal**

   6._____% means for every $100 of her loan she will pay $6.75 interest.

   **decimal**

3. Brian buys the FM Sport and within 24 months has 24,000 miles on it. At that point, he has used up _____ of his warranty.

   **fraction**

4. Raymond sees an ad for a car he would like to compare to the FM Sport. To do so, he must change the following fractions into decimals:

| **FM Sport** | **Moore Fire** |
|---|---|
| $96\frac{1}{2}$-inch wheelbase = _____ | 96.8-inch wheelbase |
| $164\frac{7}{10}$-inch overall length = _____ | 164.75-inch length |
| $66\frac{4}{5}$-inch overall width = _____ | 66.75-inch width |
| $11\frac{1}{4}$-cu.-ft. luggage space = _____ | 11.3-cu.-ft. luggage space |

5. Gloria gets a 60-month loan to buy the Sport. After one year, she has made _____ of her payments.

   **fraction**

6. Jim bargains the price of the Sport down to $10,000. Then he gets a $500 rebate. The rebate is a _____ discount from the agreed-upon price.

   **percent**

7. Jim got $2,000 for the car he traded in to buy the Sport. Jim's trade-in was a car that he had paid $8,000 for five years before. He got just _____ of his original cost.

   **percent**

8. Velma paid $810 in interest on a $9,000 loan. Velma took out the loan at _____ interest.

   **percent**

**Check your answers on page 71.**

# Increasing or Decreasing a Whole

Percent problems are often multi-step problems. Many require you to increase an original (whole) amount by adding a part to it or to decrease the original amount by subtracting a part from it.

**Directions:** A solution sentence is given for each problem. Write an arithmetic expression to match each solution sentence and then solve the problem.

Keep the coupon below in mind when solving the problems below.

**Family Charm Restaurant**
Inflation fighter
10% off your total bill
with this coupon
**Good through March 31!**

**EXAMPLE**

The Cornell family went to the Family Charm Restaurant for dinner. The bill before using the coupon was $36.80. How much was the bill after using the coupon?

**Discounted bill = original bill – amount of discount**

$$= \$36.80 - (\$36.80 \times .10)$$
$$= \$36.80 - \$3.68$$
$$= \$33.12$$

1. The Cornells' bill of $33.12 did not yet include the 5% sales tax. What was their bill after adding in tax?

   **New bill = discounted bill + amount of sales tax**

2. The Cornells' bill of $33.12 did not yet include a 15% tip either. How much did the Cornells pay for the food, tax, and service? (*Hint:* Do not include the sales tax when calculating the tip.)

   **Total amount = new bill + amount of tip**

3. Without the coupon, the total amount paid by the Cornell family would have been $36.80 plus $1.84 in sales tax plus a $5.52 tip. How much did they save by using the coupon? (*Hint:* Use the total amount found in problem 2.)

   **Amount saved = old total amount – total amount**

**Check your answers on page 71.**

# Finding Percent Increase or Decrease

Another type of multi-step percent word problem involves finding a percent increase or decrease.

**Directions:** For each problem, choose which solution sentence you will use: % increase or % decrease, and then solve the problem.

$$\% \text{ increase} = \frac{\text{Part (amount of increase)}}{\text{Whole (original amount)}}$$

$$\% \text{ decrease} = \frac{\text{Part (amount of decrease)}}{\text{Whole (original amount)}}$$

**EXAMPLE**

Judy bought a dish drainer for $4.00 that originally sold for $10.00. What percent of savings is this?

$$\% \text{ decrease} = \frac{P(\text{amount of decrease})}{W(\text{original amount})}$$
$$= \frac{(10-4)}{10}$$
$$= \frac{6}{10} = .6 = 60\%$$

1. Judy had to pay $4.24 for the $4.00 drainer, including tax. What percent of tax was added to her cost?

2. Judy went into the same store a month later and saw that the same drainer that originally sold for $10.00 now cost $11.50. What percent price increase is this?

3. Judy's friend Alice works at a store that sells the drainer for $8.00, but as an employee Alice gets it for $6.00. What is the percent of discount that Alice gets?

4. The week before the sale, the store sold 12 dish drainers. The week of the special, it sold 20 dish drainers. What was the percent increase in sales from the first week to the second?

5. Once the cost went to $11.50 for the drainers, sales went down from the regular average of 12 per week to 4 per week. What was the percent decrease in sales?

**Check your answers on page 71.**

# Percent Word Problems: Mixed Practice

Percent problems can involve finding the part, the percent, or the whole. They can also involve more than one step, such as finding percent increase, percent decrease, or the original amount.

**Directions:** On the percent circle shown with each problem, put a box around what you are trying to find: the part, the whole, or the percent. Then solve the problem. Remember that the problem might involve more than one step.

*All problems, including the example,* revolve around buying and selling homes.

**EXAMPLE**

The Fishers bought their home seven years ago for $80,000. It is now valued at $120,000. What is the percent increase in the value of their home?

$$\frac{\$120,000 - \$80,000}{\$80,000} = \frac{40,000}{80,000} = \frac{1}{2} = 50\%$$

1. The Fishers decide to sell their home. If they get their asking price of $120,000, their real estate agent will get $7,200 commission. What is the percent of commission?

2. The Fishers want to buy a new house that costs $175,000. To get the mortgage they want, they must pay a down payment of $70,000. What percent of the cost of the home is the down payment?

3. The Fishers' neighbors, the Conroys, sold their home for 17% less than their asking price. They sold the house for $152,720. What was their original asking price?

**4.** The buyers of the Conroys' home had to pay 2 points (2%) of a mortgage of $152,720 when the deal was closed. How much extra money did the buyers have to pay at the closing?

**5.** The Fishers are asking $120,000 for their home, but they have already decided they will accept a bid as low as $100,000. What percent decrease are they willing to accept?

**6.** The Fishers looked at homes in a new development. A house there will cost $160,000. The property the house sits on is 25% of that total cost. How much is the property worth?

**7.** Before the development was started, the homes were advertised at a price of $120,000. What percent increase has pushed the price up to $160,000?

**8.** After asking more questions, the Fishers find out they would have to pay 1½ points (1½%) of the $160,000 mortgage of the new home at the time of the final sale. How much would that add to the cost of the home?

**9.** The Fishers have paid off $39,000 of the mortgage on their present home. If this is 65% of the original loan, what was the total mortgage to begin with?

**Check your answers on pages 71–72.**

Book 2
**Text Pages**
145–148

## Using Estimation in Word Problems

Estimation is a useful tool for deciding which operation to use. It can also be useful for checking an answer's accuracy. Be careful, though. Some problems require more accuracy than you get when estimating.

**Directions:** In each of the following problems, an answer has been estimated. Indicate "Yes" or "No" if the estimate helps you select the exact answer from the choices given. If yes, circle the exact answer.

---

**EXAMPLE**

Matt's stock went from $20\frac{1}{2}$ dollars per share to $19\frac{3}{4}$ dollars per share in one day. How much did it go down in 24 hours?

**Estimate:** 21 dollars per share – 20 dollars per share = 1 dollar per share
one day — the next day

Does the estimate help you choose the exact answer from the choices below?      **Yes**      (**No**)

If no, why not? _Choices 1 and 2 are very close to 1._

**Exact Answer Choices**

(1) $\frac{7}{8}$

(2) $\frac{3}{4}$

(3) $\frac{5}{8}$

1. Cindy switched to the 4:00 P.M. to midnight shift to get the additional $.73 per hour for night work. How much difference will that make in her pay for a 40-hour week?

**Estimate:** $.70 × 40 = $28.00
estimated additional money per hour — hours per week

Does the estimate help you choose the exact answer from the choices below?      **Yes**      **No**

If no, why not? _____

**Exact Answer Choices**

(1) $5.84

(2) $29.20

(3) $320.00

**2.** A 9-foot by 10-foot shed is advertised as costing $575. How much does it cost per square foot?

**Estimate:** $600 ÷ 100 sq. ft. = $6.00 per sq. ft.
approximate  approximate
   cost          area

Does the estimate help you choose the exact answer from the choices below?     **Yes     No**

If no, why not? _____

**Exact Answer Choices**

**(1)** $5.75

**(2)** $6.39

**(3)** $6.50

**3.** The population of a town went from 10,600 one year to 15,688 ten years later. What was the percent of increase?

**Estimate:** 16,000 − 11,000 = 5,000; 5,000 ÷ 10,000 = 50%

Does the estimate help you choose the exact answer from the choices below?     **Yes     No**

If no, why not? _____

**Exact Answer Choices**

**(1)** 48%

**(2)** 78%

**(3)** 98%

**4.** A car can go 524.52 miles on a tank of gas. A full tank can hold 12.4 gallons of gas. How many miles can the car go on one gallon of gas?

**Estimate:** 500 ÷ 10 = 50 miles per gallon
        miles   gallons
         on       in
       1 tank    tank

Does the estimate help you choose the exact answer from the choices below?     **Yes     No**

If no, why not? _____

**Exact Answer Choices**

**(1)** 40.8 miles per gallon

**(2)** 41.2 miles per gallon

**(3)** 42.3 miles per gallon

**Check your answers on page 72.**

# Displaying and Analyzing Numerical Data

It is common to display numerical data in tables and graphs. The ability to understand and analyze data is a skill that is useful in decision making at all levels of society.

**Directions:** Analyze the data shown in each table or graph by solving the following problems.

*The example and problems 1–10 are based on the following table.*

| Dave Stieb—Pitcher | | | |
|---|---|---|---|
| Year | Wins | Losses | ERA* |
| 86 | 7 | 12 | 4.74 |
| 87 | 13 | 9 | 4.09 |
| 88 | 16 | 8 | 3.04 |
| 89 | 17 | 8 | 3.35 |
| 90 | 18 | 6 | 2.93 |

*(ERA = earned run average)

**EXAMPLE**

What was the ratio of Dave's wins to losses in 1989? __17:8__ or __$\frac{17}{8}$__

1. What was the mean (average) number of wins Dave achieved each year from 1986 through 1990? _____

2. What was Dave's median earned run average for the years 1986 through 1990?_____

3. What was the ratio of Dave's losses in 1990 to his losses in 1986?_____

4. How many more games did Dave pitch in 1990 than in 1986?_____

5. What percent increase did Dave achieve in wins in 1990 compared to 1986?_____

6. In what year did Dave's ERA go up from the previous year, even though he had more wins than in the previous year?_____

7. What was the ratio of Dave's wins to losses in 1988? (Reduce the ratio to its most simplified form.) _____ = _____

8. What percent decrease did Dave achieve in losses in 1990 compared to 1986?_____

9. By how much did Dave lower his ERA from 1986 to 1990? _____

**10.** In 1990, Dave had his lowest ERA for the five years shown. Was this also the year he had the greatest number of wins vs. least number of losses?_____

*Problems 11–15 are based on the following graph.*

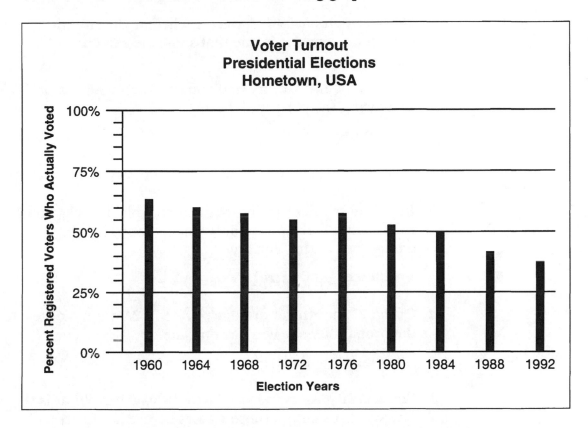

**11.** Approximately what percent of the registered voters in Hometown actually voted in the presidential election in 1964? _____

**12.** In what year was the voter turnout in Hometown for a presidential election the highest? _____

**13.** What was the approximate mean (average) percent of voter turnout in Hometown for presidential elections during the last three election years shown on the graph? _____

**14.** What was the approximate median percent of voter turnout in Hometown during the years 1960–1992 shown on the graph?_____

**15.** What was the ratio of voter turnout in Hometown in 1960 to the voter turnout in Hometown in 1988? _____

**Check your answers on page 72.**

# Probability

When we leave something to chance, we do not know for certain what the outcome will be. We can predict an outcome, however. We base a prediction on probability—how likely something is to occur.

**Directions:** *In problems 1–5*, decide whether the situation is one that is left purely to chance or if it is one that someone can control.

**EXAMPLE**

What is the probability that you can keep your cat or dog from increasing the pet population?

**Chance**    (**Control**)

(It's a controllable situation. Have your pet spayed or neutered.)

1. In a drawer full of 16 loose (unpaired) black socks and 16 loose navy socks, what is the probability that, without looking, Jack will pick out a blue sock on his first try?

    **Chance**        **Control**

2. Of the 12 monthly mortgage payments Maria makes each year, what is the probability she will pay one late?

    **Chance**        **Control**

3. Bob has 30 glasses to load into a dishwasher. What is the probability Bob will break 15 of those glasses before he finishes loading them?

    **Chance**        **Control**

4. Steve wraps up 2 packages of ground beef and 4 packages of ground turkey, all equal sizes. He forgets to label them before he puts them in the freezer. What is the probability he will take ground turkey from the freezer on his first try if he doesn't open them?

    **Chance**        **Control**

5. Marie has almost missed the 7:10 train twice this week. What is the probability she will miss the train on Friday?

    **Chance**        **Control**

**Directions:** *In problems 6–10*, give the probability in fraction and percent form. Be careful, because some probabilities are dependent on a first move.

Juliet is eating a bag of peanuts. She doesn't know it, but out of the 50 peanuts in the bag, 5 are rotten. What is the probability that the first peanut she picks will be a rotten one?

$$\frac{5 \text{ rotten}}{50 \text{ peanuts}} = \frac{1}{10} = 10\%$$

It turns out that the first 10 she eats are all right. What is the probability that the next one she eats will be rotten?

50 peanuts − 10 eaten = 40 left

$$\frac{5 \text{ rotten}}{40 \text{ peanuts}} = \frac{1}{8} = 12\frac{1}{2}\%$$

(*Note:* This was a dependent probability. It depended on how many she had already eaten.)

6. Juliet then eats 10 more peanuts, and 2 of them are rotten. Now what is the probability that the next peanut Juliet eats will be rotten?

    _____

7. Juliet keeps eating until she is left with just 2 peanuts in the bag, one of which is rotten. What is the probability that she will choose the rotten one next? _____

8. Brian looks up a telephone number his wife has written for him, but he cannot read the last number. He decides to just start trying the numbers 0 through 9. What is the probability he will dial the number correctly on his first try? _____

9. After trying the numbers 0 through 4 and getting the wrong telephone number each time, Brian dials a 5. What is the probability he will then get the right telephone number? _____

10. There are 100 guests at a benefit dinner. The names of all the guests are put in a hat to draw for a door prize. What is the probability that one of seven guests from one family will get the door prize?

    _____

**Check your answers on page 72.**

# POST-TEST FOR BOOK 1 AND BOOK 2

**Directions:** The following problems test the skills you reviewed in this workbook. For each problem, choose one answer from the five choices given.

1. Jackie purchased an 18-speed mountain bike on an employee discount. She paid $300 for the bike, which was priced at $400. What percent did she get as an employee?

   **(1)** 20%

   **(2)** 25%

   **(3)** $33\frac{1}{3}$%

   **(4)** 75%

   **(5)** 80%

2. Gloria is going to plant a row of tulip bulbs in a $4\frac{1}{2}$-foot flower bed in front of her house. If she needs to keep them 6 inches apart, how many tulip bulbs can she plant in this space? (*Hint:* Draw a picture.)

   **(1)** 2 bulbs

   **(2)** 8 bulbs

   **(3)** 9 bulbs

   **(4)** 10 bulbs

   **(5)** 27 bulbs

3. Mr. and Mrs. Stevens want to purchase a home that costs $120,000. They are told that at the closing they will need to have a 20% down payment and $2\frac{1}{2}$ points ($2\frac{1}{2}$% of the mortgage, which equals $2,400). How much money will the Stevenses need to bring to the closing?

   **(1)** $2,400

   **(2)** $2,700

   **(3)** $24,000

   **(4)** $26,400

   **(5)** $27,000

**4.** George earned $7.25 per hour on first shift for 18 months without getting a raise. He switched to second shift and started at $8.10 per hour for the same job. How much more does George now earn in a 40-hour week on second shift than he did on first shift?

(1) $324

(2) $290

(3) $85

(4) $34

(5) $.85

**5.** An advertisement for a restaurant chain says it now has 256 locations in 16 states. Last year the same chain had 210 restaurants in 14 states. What was the increase in the average number of restaurants per state?

(1) 46 restaurants

(2) 16 restaurants

(3) 15 restaurants

(4) 2 restaurants

(5) 1 restaurant

**6.** Manuel traveled 127 miles Friday, 98 miles Saturday, and 150 miles on Sunday before he used up a full tank of gasoline. His car has a 12.5-gallon gas tank. What kind of gas mileage (miles per gallon) does his car get?

(1) 387.5 mpg

(2) 375 mpg

(3) 125 mpg

(4) 30 mpg

(5) 10.16 mpg

**7.** Three friends are renting a townhouse and sharing all the expenses equally. The rent is $891 per month, utilities run $210 per month, and food costs $420 each month. How much a month does each friend pay?

(1) $4,563

(2) $1,521

(3) $891

(4) $507

(5) $297

**Next page** ➙

**8.** Advertisements for a new brand of "light" margarine say it has 40% fewer calories than the most popular brand. If the new margarine contains 60 calories per tablespoon, how many calories per tablespoon does the most popular brand contain?

**(1)** 100 calories

**(2)** 96 calories

**(3)** 84 calories

**(4)** 36 calories

**(5)** 24 calories

**9.** Michael's electric bill last month was $150. This month Michael reduced his electric usage and decreased his bill by 12%. What was his bill for this month?

**(1)** $168

**(2)** $162

**(3)** $138

**(4)** $132

**(5)** $18

**10.** How much change should you get from a $20 bill if you bought a box of facial tissues for $.89, some cough drops for $.59, and a box of cold tablets for $3.19 and paid $.30 tax on the purchase?

**(1)** $15.33

**(2)** $15.03

**(3)** $14.03

**(4)** $8.83

**(5)** $4.97

**11.** Joan can get airline fares for 25% of the regular price through her employer. If she paid $80 for her last flight, what would have been the regular fare?

**(1)** $20

**(2)** $25

**(3)** $60

**(4)** $100

**(5)** $320

**12.** A baseball player had the following batting averages for the past five seasons: .297, .305, .286, .290, and .279. What was his overall batting average for the five seasons?

**(1)** 7.285

**(2)** 1.457

**(3)** .364

**(4)** .291

**(5)** .290

**13.** Betty takes an aerobics class three times a week. Each class is 45 minutes long. She also spends 20 minutes 6 days a week walking a total of $1\frac{1}{2}$ miles. How many hours per week does she spend exercising?

**(1)** 65 hours

**(2)** $9\frac{1}{4}$ hours

**(3)** $7\frac{1}{4}$ hours

**(4)** $4\frac{1}{4}$ hours

**(5)** $1\frac{1}{4}$ hours

**14.** Ida got a $.75-per-hour raise after first six months on her job. If she was earning $5.15 per hour when first started, what does she now earn every 40-hour week?

**(1)** $236

**(2)** $206

**(3)** $30

**(4)** $5.90

**(5)** Not enough information is given.

**Next page →**

*Problems 15–17 are based on the following recipe.*

---

**Mince Mix**

1 egg $\frac{1}{4}$ teaspoon pepper
$\frac{2}{3}$ cup chopped onion 2 pounds hamburger
$1\frac{1}{2}$ teaspoons Italian seasoning $\frac{3}{4}$ cup bread crumbs
$\frac{1}{2}$ teaspoon salt

Blend ingredients and bake in a loaf pan for 1 hour at 350°, or roll into balls and cook 35 minutes on medium heat on the stove. Serves 6.

---

**15.** If you change the recipe to make just three servings, how much Italian seasoning would you use?

**(1)** $\frac{1}{2}$ tsp.

**(2)** $\frac{3}{4}$ tsp.

**(3)** 1 tsp.

**(4)** $1\frac{1}{2}$ tsp.

**(5)** 3 tsp.

**16.** How much longer does the mince loaf take to cook than the mince balls?

**(1)** 5 minutes

**(2)** 15 minutes

**(3)** 25 minutes

**(4)** 34 minutes

**(5)** 65 minutes

**17.** John wants to make enough to serve 6 people but has only $\frac{1}{8}$ cup of bread crumbs. How much more does he need?

**(1)** $1\frac{3}{8}$ cups

**(2)** $\frac{7}{8}$ cup

**(3)** $\frac{3}{4}$ cup

**(4)** $\frac{5}{8}$ cup

**(5)** $\frac{1}{4}$ cup

*Problems 18–20 are based on the following graph.*

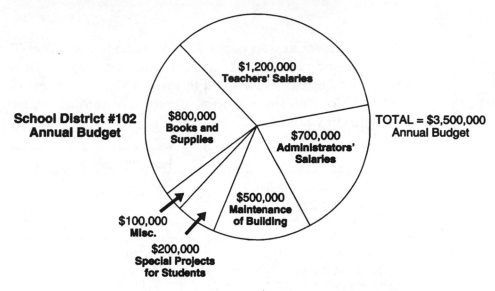

18. What percent of the total annual budget are administrators' salaries?

    (1) .2%

    (2) 2%

    (3) 20%

    (4) 200%

    (5) Not enough information is given.

19. Which of the following budget categories is ⅐ of the total annual budget?

    (1) administrators' salaries

    (2) books and supplies

    (3) special projects

    (4) maintenance of buildings

    (5) miscellaneous

20. The school district's budget represents 10% of the county's entire annual budget. What is the county's total annual budget?

    (1) $350,000

    (2) $3,500,000

    (3) $35,000,000

    (4) $350,000,000

    (5) $3,500,000,000

**Check your answers on page 72.**

# POST-TEST EVALUATION CHART

Use the answer key on pages 72–73 to check your Post-Test answers. Then in the second column of this chart, find the number of each question you missed and circle it. This will tell you which chapters you might need to review before you move on to one of Contemporary's higher level mathematics books.

| Skill | Item Number | Number Correct |
|---|---|---|
| Special Topics in Math<br>Book 1, Chapter 6<br>Pages 134–164 | 2, 5, 7, 16 | ___/4 |
| Word-Problem Skills<br>Book 2, Chapter 1<br>Pages 2–29 | 13 | ___/1 |
| Decimal Skills<br>Book 2, Chapter 3<br>Pages 34–64 | 4, 6, 10, 12, 14 | ___/5 |
| Common Fraction Skills<br>Book 2, Chapter 4<br>Pages 66–112 | 15, 17 | ___/2 |
| Percent Skills<br>Book 2, Chapter 5<br>Pages 114–141 | 1, 3, 8, 9, 11 | ___/5 |
| Special Topics in Math<br>Book 2, Chapter 6<br>Pages 142–172 | 18, 19, 20 | ___/3 |
| | Total Correct | ___/20 |

# ANSWER KEY

## WHOLE NUMBERS

### Rounding Whole Numbers and Money
### Page 4

1. 61,000

2. 76,000

3. 58,000

4. 41,000

5. 600

6. 200

7. 300

8. 900

9. $2.00

10. $29.00

11. $6,000.00

12. $700.00

### Writing Dollars and Cents
### Page 5

```
JoAnn Fellows                                    589
363 Hibernia Dr.
Carroll, MD 21000                        AUG. 6 19 9X
Pay to the Order of  People's Electricity   $ 47.53
Forty-seven and 53/100 ──────────── Dollars

Citizens' Bank
                                  JoAnn Fellows
0421873090      444  0999  6  589
```

```
JoAnn Fellows                                    590
363 Hibernia Dr.
Carroll, MD 21000                        AUG. 6 19 9X
Pay to the Order of  Home Management, Inc. $ 375.00
Three hundred seventy-five and no/100 ── Dollars

Citizens' Bank
                                  JoAnn Fellows
0421873090      444  0999  6  590
```

```
JoAnn Fellows                                    591
363 Hibernia Dr.
Carroll, MD 21000                        AUG. 6 19 9X
Pay to the Order of  Tone Telephone     $ 28.66
Twenty-eight and 66/100 ──────────── Dollars

Citizens' Bank
                                  JoAnn Fellows
0421873090      444  0999  6  591
```

## ADDITION SKILLS

### Identifying What You Are to Find
### Page 6

1. How much will tuition be per credit hour next semester?

   | $39.00 (this semester) | $ 9.00 |
   |---|---|
   | + 9.00 (raise) | + 39.00 |
   | $48.00 (next semester) | $48.00 |

2. How much does Mark earn each week?

   | $466.00 (full-time job) | $466.00 |
   |---|---|
   | +123.00 (weekend job) | +123.00 |
   | $589.00 (total earnings) | $589.00 |

3. What temperature will it probably be in Baltimore when it is 48° in Chicago?

   | 48° | 10° |
   |---|---|
   | + 10° | + 48° |
   | 58° | 58° |

4. How long does it take this train to travel from Harrisburg to Minneapolis?

   | 14 hours | 9 hours |
   |---|---|
   | +9 hours | + 14 hours |
   | 23 hours | 23 hours |

5. If the biscuits take 12 minutes to bake, what time will they be ready?

   | 6:15 P.M. | 12 minutes |
   |---|---|
   | + 12 minutes | + 6:15 P.M. |
   | 6:27 P.M. | 6:27 P.M. |

6. Find how much it cost the Scotts to own and operate the car that month.

   | $271.10 (car payment) | $ 56.60 |
   |---|---|
   | 113.87 (maintenance) | 62.50 |
   | 62.50 (insurance) | 113.87 |
   | + 56.60 (gas) | + 271.10 |
   | $504.07 (total for month) | $504.07 |

### Finding Necessary Information
### Page 7

Your wording may vary, but your answers should contain the same information as the following answers.

1. Necessary information: cost of a tuna sandwich and an order of cheese sticks.

   $3.75 (tuna sandwich)
   + 3.50 (cheese sticks)
   $7.25 (Manny's bill)

**2.** Necessary information: cost of chicken wings, a club sandwich, a cola, and a coffee.

$3.95 (chicken wings)
4.95 (club sandwich)
1.00 (coffee)
+ 1.00 (cola)
$10.90 (Thomas's bill)

**3.** Necessary information: bill for $66.50, a $10.00 tip.

$66.50 (bill)
+ 10.00 (tip)
$76.50 (total)

## SUBTRACTION SKILLS

### Whole Numbers and Money
### Page 8

**1.** $692.28 (federal)
− 138.48 (state)
$553.80

**2.** $4,615.38 (this year)
− 3,998.15 (last year)
$617.23

**3.** $553.43 (check)
− 5.50 (charge)
$547.93

**4.** $547.93 (received from currency exchange)
− 25.00 (put in savings account)
$522.93

**5.** $18.50 (health)
− 11.15 (medicare)
$7.35

### Deciding When to Add or Subtract
### Page 9

**1. (2)** 1,050 + 950 = 2,000

**2. (1)** 88° − 67° = 21°

**3. (1)** $75.68 − $4.82 = $70.86

**4. (2)** 8:00 P.M. + 2 hours = 10:00 P.M.

### Addition and Subtraction:
### Information Needed
### Pages 10–11

Your wording may vary, but your answers should contain the same information as the following answers.

**1. a.** Addition

**b.** Information needed: cost of one month's payment ($295), number of months being figured (3).

**c.** Solution: $295 (January)
295 (February)
+ 295 (March)
$885 (three-month total)

**2. a.** Subtraction

**b.** Information needed: Total cost of loan ($14,160), list price ($12,679), cash rebate ($555).

**c.** Solution:
$12,679 (list price)     $14,160 (loan)
− 555 (rebate)          − 12,124 (cash)
$12,124 (cash price)    $ 2,036 (less)

**3. a.** Subtraction

**b.** Information needed: one year of payments (12), total number of payments (48).

**c.** Solution: 48 payments
− 12 payments
36 payments

**4. a.** Addition

**b.** Information needed: distance from Minneapolis to Yellowstone (1,109 miles), distance from Yellowstone to Glacier (367 miles).

**c.** Solution: 1,109 miles
+ 367 miles
1,476 total miles

**5. a.** Subtraction

**b.** Information needed: travel time from Minneapolis to Yellowstone (20 hours), travel time from Yellowstone to Glacier (7 hours).

**c.** Solution: 20 hours
− 7 hours
13 hours

**6. a.** Addition

**b.** Information needed: travel time from Glacier to Yellowstone (7 hours), travel time from Yellowstone to Minneapolis (20 hours).

**c.** Solution: 20 hours
+ 7 hours
27 hours total

**7. a.** Subtraction

**b.** Information needed: price of cat food ($2.59 each), value of coupon ($.75).

**c.** Solution: $2.59
− .75
$1.84 cost using coupon

**8. a.** Addition

    **b.** Information needed: prices of bathroom tissue (99 cents), 2 packages of rolls (79 cents + 79 cents), applesauce (99 cents).

    **c.** Solution:  $.99
                    .79
                    .79
             + .99
        $3.56 total for items on list

## MULTIPLICATION SKILLS

### Using Approximation in Word Problems
### Page 12

**1. Operation:** multiply
    **Substitute:** $600.00 for $598.90
    **Estimate:** $600 × 12 = $7,200
    **Exact answer: (3)** $7,186.80

**2. Operation:** add
    **Substitute:** 1,000 for 982; 1,000 for 998; 1,000 for 1,010
    **Estimate:** 1,000 + 1,000 + 1,000 = 3,000
    **Exact answer: (2)** 2,990

**3. Operation:** subtract
    **Substitute:** 50.00 for 50.25
    **Estimate:** $75.00 – $50.00 = $25.00
    **Exact answer: (2)** $24.75

### Solving Word Problems
### Page 13

**1. a.** Estimate

    **b.** A dress shirt costs about $20. A pair of boots costs about $16. A pair of slacks costs about $17.
    $20 + $16 + $17 = $53, so Ellen can get the slacks.

**2. a.** Exact

    **b.** $25.99 (per sweater) × 2 = $51.98
    $51.98 + $3.12 (tax) = $55.10

**3. a.** Exact

    **b.** $49.99 (regular price) – $25.99 (sale price) = $24.00 (savings per sweater)
    $24.00 × 2 = $48.00 (total savings)

## DIVISION SKILLS

### Division Word Problems
### Page 14

**1.** $5\overline{)23}$ (4R3)

Answer: 5 cars (because remaining 3 children must ride in a fifth car)

**2.** $8\overline{)30}$ (3R6)

Answer: 4 packages (because 6 hamburgers are left without buns if you buy just 3 packages)

**3.** $12\overline{)68}$ (5R8)

Answer: 6 boxes (otherwise she will have 8 names left on her card list without cards)

**4.** $350\overline{)750}$ (2R50)

Answer: 3 times (in order to go the remaining 50 miles)

**5.** $.50\overline{)12.47}$ (24R47)

Answer: 25 certificates (in order to cover the whole amount, including the remaining $.47)

**6.** $2\overline{)13}$ (6R1)

Answer: 6 (cannot make another batch with only 1 cup)

### Deciding When to Multiply or Divide
### Page 15

    **1. (2)** Division: $222

    **2. (1)** Multiplication: $4,608

    **3. (1)** Multiplication: 72 miles

    **4. (2)** Division: $4.67

### Solving Word Problems
### Pages 16–17

    **1. Information needed:** total loss for period ($165,000), number of months (4).
    <u>X</u> division

    **2. Information needed:** actual loss ($165,000), expected loss ($490,000).
    <u>X</u> subtraction

3. **Information needed:** first 4-month loss ($440,000), second 4-month loss ($165,000). X addition

4. **Information needed:** number of cookies in a box (12), number of boxes (11). X multiplication

5. **Information needed:** cost for one box ($2.59), number of boxes (11). X multiplication

## Solving Word Problems—More Practice Pages 18–19

1. **Operation:** add
   **Estimate:** 30 (won) + 20 (lost) = 50 games played

2. **Operation:** subtract
   **Estimate:** 150 (second) – 120 (first) = 30 pins

3. **Operation:** divide
   **Estimate:** 300 (points) ÷ 3 (games) = 100 average each game

4. **Operation:** divide
   **Estimate:** 2,400 (points) ÷ 12 (games) = 200 average each game

5. **Operation:** add
   **Estimate:** 18 (lost so far) + 12 (of their last 15) = 30 games lost in all

6. **Operation:** multiply
   **Estimate:** 3 (minimum lines) × $20 (per line) = $60

7. **Operation:** multiply
   **Estimate:** 5 (lines) × $5 (per line) = $25

8. **Operation:** subtract
   **Estimate:** $100 – $25 = $75

9. **Operation:** divide
   **Estimate:** $60 (total) ÷ 3 (days) = $20

10. **Operation:** add
    **Estimate:** $85 + $60 + $40 = $185

## SPECIAL TOPICS IN MATH—BOOK 1

### Multi-Step Word Problems Pages 20–21

1. **Solution sentence:** Difference between top weekly pay of carpenter and top weekly pay of laborer = 40-hour pay of carpenter – 40-hour pay of laborer.

**Step 1:** Multiply to find weekly pay of each
$22 × 40 hr. = $880 (carpenter)
$16 × 40 hr. = $640 (laborer)
**Step 2:** Subtract to find the difference in weekly pay.
$880 – $640 = $240 difference

2. **Solution sentence:** Take-home pay = 80-hour pay of mason – $695 deductions.

**Step 1:** Multiply to find 80-hour pay
$22.50 × 80 hr. = $1,800
**Step 2:** Subtract to take out deductions.
$1,800 – $695 = $1,105 take-home pay

3. **Solution sentence:** Difference in pay per hour = hourly wage for top-paid carpenter – hourly wage for Lea.

**Step 1:** Divide to find Lea's hourly wage.
$430 ÷ 40 hr. = $10.75 per hour
**Step 2:** Subtract to find the difference between wages.
$22 – $10.75 = $11.25 difference per hour in pay

4. **Solution sentence:** Yearly earnings = number of hours worked × wages per hour.

**Step 1:** Multiply to find the number of hours worked.
40 × 50 = 2,000 hours
**Step 2:** Multiply to find how much Martin earned.
2,000 × $16 = $32,000

5. **Solution sentence:** January "losses" = hours not worked × wages per hour.

**Step 1:** Subtract to find the difference in hours worked.
160 – 100 = 60 hours
**Step 2:** Multiply to find the additional amount of money Carl would have earned.
60 × $22.50 = $1,350

### Estimation with Measurement Page 22

1. (3) 36 ounces

2. (1) ginger ale

3. (3) 135 feet

4. (2) 2 meters

5. (1) 4 min., 33.9 sec.

## Measurement Problems
## Page 23

1. 250 ml )1.5 l  = 250 ml )1,500 ml   $\overset{\text{6 servings}}{}$

2. half liter = 500 ml

   250 ml )500 ml   $\overset{\text{2 servings}}{}$

   120 calories ÷ 2 = 60 calories per serving

3.   17 lb.  8 oz.  =  16 lb. 24 oz.
   <br>  – 8 lb. 14 oz.  =  – 8 lb. 14 oz.
   <br>                            8 lb. 10 oz.

4. 8 lb. 14 oz.
   <br>  ×  2

   16 lb. 28 oz. = 17 lb. 12 oz.  No, the baby's weight did not double. He weighed only 17 lb. 8 oz. at 6 months.

5.   10 km         =     9 km 1,000 m
   <br>  – 2 km 300 m     – 2 km   300 m
   <br>                       7 km 700 m from finish

6.   2 km 300 m
   <br> + 2 km 700 m
   <br>   4 km 1,000 m = 5 km

## Perimeter, Area, and Volume
## Page 24

1. a. perimeter

   b. (2 × 9 ft.) + (2 × 11 ft.) = 18 ft. + 22 ft. = **40 ft.**

2. a. area

   b. 9 ft. × 8 ft. = **72 sq. ft.**

3. a. volume

   b. 3 in. × 2 in. × 1 in. = **6 cu. in.**

## Squares, Cubes, and Square Roots
## Page 25

**Challenge 1:**

a. 8

b. 100

c. 10 ( $\sqrt{100}$ )

d. 64 (10 – 2 = 8; $8^2$ = 64)

e. 36 (64 ÷ 2 = 32 + 4 = 36)

f. 6 ( $\sqrt{36}$ )

g. 2 (6 ÷ 3 = 2)

**Challenge 2:**

a. 3 ( $\sqrt{9}$ )

b. 27 ( $3^3$ )

c. 900 (27 + 3 = 30; $30^2$ = 900)

d. 100 (9 )900 )

e. 9 ( $\sqrt{100}$ = 10; 10 – 1 = 9)

**Challenge 3:**

a. 25 (13 × 2 = 26; 26 – 1 = 25)

b. 5 ( $\sqrt{25}$ )

c. 121 ($5^3$ = 125; 125 – 4 = 121)

d. 12 ( $\sqrt{121}$ = 11; 11 + 1 = 12)

e. 144 ( $12^2$ )

f. 169 (144 + $5^2$ = 144 + 25 = 169)

g. 13 ( $\sqrt{169}$ )

## SKILLS REVIEW

## Steps in Solving Word Problems
## Page 28

**Step 2.** I need: $2.59 (regular price), $.75 (coupon)

**Step 3.** The operation: subtraction

**Step 4.** Answer: $1.84

**Step 5.** less than; $1.84 is less than $2.59, so, yes, it checks.

## Using Estimates to Check Answers
## Page 29

1. a. Add

   b. $16,000 + $24,000 = $40,000

   c. No

   d. $16,398 + $23,740 = $40,138

2. a. Divide

   b. $24,000 ÷ 12 = $2,000 per month

   c. No

   d. $23,740 ÷ 12 = $1,978.33

3. a. Subtract

   b. $18,000 – $16,000 = $2,000 raise

   c. Yes, $1,727 is close to $2,000.

### Expressions and Order of Operations
### Page 30

1. **(2)** $55 + (15 \times 34) = 55 + (510) = 565$

2. **(2)** $75 + (24 \times 40) = 75 + (960) = 1,035$

3. **(3)** $25 + (36 \times 10) + 150 = 25 + (360) + 150 = 535$

## DECIMALS, FRACTIONS, AND PERCENTS

### Numbers Smaller than 1
### Page 31

1. a. **(7)**       f. **(10)**

   b. **(8)**       g. **(1)**

   c. **(6)**       h. **(5)**

   d. **(2)**       i. **(3)**

   e. **(9)**       j. **(4)**

2. $\frac{5}{1,000}$

3. $\frac{8}{100}$

4. $\frac{52}{100}$

5. $\$.05$

6. $\$.50$

## DECIMAL SKILLS

### Comparing and Ordering Decimal Fractions
### Page 32

1. .189, .198, .209, .270

2. $\$.05$, $\$.0525$, $\$.06$, $\$.065$

3. .098, .25, .5, .75

4. .0538, .061, .1175, .12

5. 398.39, 398.780, 398.825, 398.9

6. $\$1.289$, $\$1.30$, $\$1.379$, $\$1.498$

### Rounding Decimal Fractions
### Page 33

1. $\$.07$ for Whitcomb's, $\$.07$ for Season's, $\boxed{\$.06 \text{ for Jane Newman's}}$

2. $\$.93$ for Regent's, $\boxed{\$.84 \text{ for Purity,}}$ $\$.94$ for Health-Tech

3. $\boxed{\$.77 \text{ for Hall's,}}$ $\$.78$ for Precious, $\$.78$ for Glory

4. $\boxed{\$.28 \text{ for Tasty Treat,}}$ $\$.29$ for Crunchy Crisp, $\$.29$ for Sudden Surprise

5. $\$1.38$, $\$1.40$, $\boxed{\$1.31}$

### Solving Math Word Problems
### Pages 34–35

1. **(1)** $2.83 - 2.50$

2. **(1)** $(3.03 + 2.97) + 2$

3. **(1)** $37.75 + 40.6 + 30.5 + 40.6$

4. **(3)** $\$10.80 \times 7.25$

5. **(2)** $.07 - .058$

6. **(3)** $.212 \times .306$

### Solving Multi-Step Word Problems
### Pages 36–37

1. $(\$9.95 - \$9.75)$
   $\$.20 \times 2 = \mathbf{\$.40}$

2. Charges by Choice
   $\$52.00 + \$35.00 = \mathbf{\$87.00}$

3. $(\$26.00 + 10 \text{ lb.})$
   $\$4.39 - \$2.60 = \mathbf{\$1.79}$

4. $(2 \times 60 \text{ mg})$
   $120 \text{ mg} + 49.75 \text{ mg} = \mathbf{169.75 \text{ mg}}$

5. 20 mg
   $5.45 \text{ mg} + 20 \text{ mg} = \mathbf{25.45 \text{ mg}}$

6. amount in Complete Vitamin Tablet
   $31.2 \text{ mg} - 25.2 \text{ mg} = \mathbf{6 \text{ mg}}$

## COMMON FRACTION SKILLS

### Comparing Common Fractions
### Page 38

1. $\frac{3}{4} = \frac{12}{16}$, $\frac{7}{16} = \frac{7}{16}$, $\frac{1}{2} = \frac{8}{16}$, $\frac{3}{8} = \frac{6}{16}$
   So, the right one is $\frac{3}{8}$.

2. $\frac{9}{16} = \frac{18}{32}$, $\frac{7}{8} = \frac{28}{32}$, $\frac{1}{4} = \frac{8}{32}$, $\frac{5}{32} = \frac{5}{32}$  So, the closest to a half-inch is $\frac{9}{16}$. The smallest is $\frac{5}{32}$.

3. $\frac{5}{16} = \frac{5}{16}$, $\frac{1}{4} = \frac{4}{16}$, $\frac{3}{16} = \frac{3}{16}$, $\frac{1}{8} = \frac{2}{16}$  So, the answer is Defense at $\frac{5}{16}$.

### Finding What Fraction a Part Is of a Whole
### Page 39

1. $\frac{13}{52} = \frac{1}{4}$

2. $\frac{28}{52} = \frac{7}{13}$

3. $\frac{600}{2,000} = \frac{3}{10}$

4. $\frac{200}{2,000} = \frac{1}{10}$

5. $\frac{250}{2,000} = \frac{1}{8}$

6. $\frac{400}{2,000} = \frac{1}{5}$

7. $\frac{50}{1,760} = \frac{5}{176}$

8. $\frac{100}{1,760} = \frac{5}{88}$

9. $\frac{880}{1,760} = \frac{1}{2}$

10. $\frac{8}{32} = \frac{1}{4}$

11. $\frac{16}{32} = \frac{1}{2}$

12. $\frac{6}{32} = \frac{3}{16}$

## Solving Fraction Word Problems
## Pages 40–41

1. Whole number equation: $865 \times 1 = 865$ miles
   Solution: $865 \times \frac{9}{16} = 486\frac{9}{16}$ miles

2. Whole number equation: $2 - 1 = 1$ inch
   Solution: $1\frac{3}{4} - \frac{9}{16} = 1\frac{3}{16}$ inches

3. Whole number equation: $1 + 1 = 2$ inch
   Solution: $1\frac{3}{16} + 1\frac{3}{8} = 1\frac{19}{16} = 2\frac{3}{16}$ inches

4. Whole number equation: $865 \times 2 = 1,730$ miles
   Solution: $865 \times 2\frac{3}{16} = 1,892\frac{3}{16}$ miles

5. Whole number equation: $4 - 1 = 3$
   Solution: $3\frac{1}{2} - \frac{5}{8} = \frac{28}{8} - \frac{5}{8} = \frac{23}{8} = 2\frac{7}{8}$

## Comparison Word Problems
## Pages 42–43

1. $2\frac{3}{8}$, because $2\frac{3}{8} = 2.3750$, $2\frac{7}{16} = 2.4375$, $2\frac{1}{2} = 2.5000$, $2.75 = 2.7500$

2. $4\frac{1}{4}\%$, because $4.125\% = 4.125\%$, $4\,1/7\% = 4.143\%$, $4.20\% = 4.200\%$, $4\frac{1}{4}\% = 4.250\%$

3. Recipe A 24 ounces of chicken, because 24 ounces = 1.5 pounds and $2\frac{3}{8}$ pounds = 2.375 pounds

4. $\frac{1}{8}$-inch, because $\frac{1}{8} = .125$

5. Yes, the coleslaw, because $.75 = \frac{3}{4}$, $1\frac{1}{2}$ lb. = 1.50 lb., $\frac{3}{4}$ lb. = .75 lb., 16 oz. = 1.0 lb.

6. All three were the same.

7. .93 mile, because $.62 \times 1.5 = .93$

## Decimal and Fraction Multi-Step Word Problems
## Pages 44–45

1. Ed Brenner's hours
   $6\frac{1}{4} - (\frac{3}{4} + 1\frac{1}{4} + 2\frac{1}{4}) =$
   $6\frac{1}{4} - 4\frac{1}{4} = 2$

2. divide
   $\$31.50 \div (\frac{1}{2} + 2 + 1\frac{3}{4} + \frac{1}{4}) =$
   $\$31.50 \div 4\frac{1}{2} = \$7.00$

3. Number of overtime hours each week
   $(\frac{1}{2} + \frac{1}{4} + \frac{3}{4} + \frac{1}{2} + \frac{1}{4}) \times 4 =$
   $2\frac{1}{4} \times 4 = 9$ hours

4. (3) $(\frac{3}{4} + 1\frac{1}{2} + 2\frac{1}{4} + 1\frac{1}{2} + 2 + 2\frac{1}{4}) - (\frac{1}{2} + 1\frac{1}{4} + 2 + 1\frac{3}{4})$

5. (1) $(\$5.75 \times 40) + \$8.63 \times (\frac{1}{2} + \frac{1}{4} + \frac{3}{4} + \frac{1}{2} + \frac{1}{4})$

## PERCENT SKILLS

### Word Problems: Percents, Decimals, and Fractions
### Pages 46–47

1. $\frac{3}{10}$ or 30%

2. 6.75%
   $6.90
   6.75%

3. $\frac{2}{3}$

4. 96.5
   164.70
   66.80
   11.25

5. $\frac{1}{5}$

6. 5%

7. 25%

8. 9%

### Increasing or Decreasing a Whole
### Page 48

1. $\$33.12 + (33.12 \times .05) = 33.12 + 1.66 = \$34.78$

2. $\$34.78 + (33.12 \times .15) = 34.78 + 4.97 = \$39.75$

3. $(\$36.80 + \$1.84 + \$5.52) - \$39.75 = \$4.41$

### Finding Percent Increase or Decrease
### Page 49

1. Percent increase
   $\frac{4.24 - 4.00}{4.00} = \frac{.24}{4.00} = .06 = 6\%$

2. Percent increase
   $\frac{11.50 - 10.00}{10.00} = \frac{1.50}{10.00} = .15 = 15\%$

3. Percent decrease
   $\frac{8.00 - 6.00}{8.00} = \frac{2.00}{8.00} = .25 = 25\%$

4. Percent increase
   $\frac{20 - 12}{12} = \frac{8}{12} = 66\frac{2}{3}\%$

5. Percent decrease
   $\frac{12 - 4}{12} = \frac{8}{12} = 66\frac{2}{3}\%$

### Percent Word Problems: Mixed Practice
### Pages 50–51

1. % $\frac{7,200}{\% \times 120,000} = \frac{3}{50} = 6\%$

2. % $\frac{70,000}{\% \times 175,000} = \frac{2}{5} = 40\%$

3. W $\frac{152,720}{(100\% - 17\%) \times W} = \frac{152,720}{.83} = \$184,000$

4. P $\frac{P}{2\% \times 152,720} = .02 \times 152,720 = \$3,054.40$

**5.** % $\dfrac{120,000 - 100,000}{\% \times 120,000} = \dfrac{20,000}{120,000} = \dfrac{1}{6} = 16\frac{2}{3}\%$

**6.** P $\dfrac{P}{25\% \times 160,000} = .25 \times 160,000 = \$40,000$

**7.** % $\dfrac{160,000 - 120,000}{\% \times 120,000} = \dfrac{40,000}{120,000} = \dfrac{1}{3} = 33\frac{1}{3}\%$

**8.** P $\dfrac{P}{1\frac{1}{2}\% \times 160,000} = .015 \times 160,000 = \$2,400$

**9.** W $\dfrac{39,000}{65\% \times W} = \dfrac{39,000}{.65} = \$60,000$

## SPECIAL TOPICS IN MATH—BOOK 2

### Using Approximation in Word Problems
### Pages 52–53

**1.** Yes, choice (2) is closest to the approximate.

**2.** No, the answer choices are too close.

**3.** Yes, choice (1) is closest to the approximate.

**4.** No, the answer choices are too close.

### Displaying and Analyzing Numerical Data
### Pages 54–55

**1.** $(7 + 13 + 16 + 17 + 18) \div 5 = 14.2$

**2.** 3.35 (Arrange values from least to greatest and choose the middle value.)

**3.** 6:12

**4.** $(18 + 6) - (7 + 12) = 5$

**5.** $\dfrac{18 - 7}{7} = 1.57 = 157\%$

**6.** 1989

**7.** 16:8 or 2:1

**8.** $\dfrac{12 - 6}{12} = \dfrac{6}{12} = \dfrac{1}{2} = 50\%$

**9.** 1.81

**10.** Yes

**11.** 59% (Answers between 55% and 65% correct.)

**12.** 1960

**13.** $(50 + 41 + 38) \div 3 = 43$ (Answers between 40 and 50 are correct.)

**14.** 60% (Answers close to 60% are correct.)

**15.** 63:41 (Answers within 5 of either number are correct.)

### Probability
### Pages 56–57

**1.** Chance

**2.** Control

**3.** Control

**4.** Chance

**5.** Control

**6.** 10 + 10 peanuts eaten = 20 eaten; 50 − 20 = 30 yet to eat; 5 rotten altogether − 2 already eaten = 3 rotten left; $\dfrac{3}{30} = \dfrac{1}{10} = 10\%$

**7.** $\dfrac{1}{2} = 50\%$

**8.** $\dfrac{1}{10} = 10\%$

**9.** 10 numbers to begin with − 5 numbers dialed = 5 to go; $\dfrac{1}{5} = 20\%$

**10.** $\dfrac{7}{100} = 7\%$

## POST-TEST ANSWER KEY

### Pages 58–63

**1.** (2) 25%
$\dfrac{400 - 300}{400}$

**2.** (4) 10 bulbs
$4\frac{1}{2}$ ft. = 54 in.
54 ÷ 6 = 9 six-inch spaces + 1 bulb to start the row

**3.** (4) $26,400
$120,000 \times 20\% + \$2,400 = \$24,000 + \$2,400 = \$26,400$

**4.** (4) $34
$(\$8.10 - \$7.25) \times 40 = \$.85 \times 40 = \$34$

**5.** (5) 1 restaurant
$\dfrac{256}{16} = 16, \dfrac{210}{14} = 15$
16 − 15 = 1

**6.** (4) 30 mpg
$(127 + 98 + 150) \div 12.5 = 375 \div 12.5 = 30$

**7.** (4) $507
$(\$891 + \$210 + \$420) \div 3 = \$1,521 \div 3 = \$507$

**8.** (1) 100 calories
$\dfrac{60}{60\% \times W} = \dfrac{60}{.6} = 100$

**9.** (4) $132
$\$150 - (\$150 \times 12\%) = \$150 - \$18 = \$132$

**10.** (2) $15.03
$\$20.00 - (\$.89 + \$.59 + \$3.19 + \$.30) = \$20.00 - \$4.97 = \$15.03$

**11.** (5) $320
$\dfrac{\$80}{25\% \times W} = \dfrac{\$80}{.25} = \$320$

**12. (4)** .291

(.297 + .305 + .286 + .290 + .279) ÷ 5 = 1.457 ÷ 5 = .291

**13. (4)** $4\frac{1}{4}$ hours

$$\frac{(45 \times 3) + (20 \times 6)}{60} = \frac{135 + 120}{60} = 4\frac{1}{4}$$

**14. (1)** $236

($5.15 + $.75) × 40 = $5.90 × 40 = $236

**15. (2)** $\frac{3}{4}$ tsp.

$1\frac{1}{2} \times \frac{1}{2} = \frac{3}{2} \times \frac{1}{2} = \frac{3}{4}$

**16. (3)** 25 minutes

1 hr. = 60 min.; 60 − 35 = 25

**17. (4)** $\frac{5}{8}$ cup

$\frac{3}{4} - \frac{1}{8} = \frac{6}{8} - \frac{1}{8} = \frac{5}{8}$

**18. (3)** 20%

$$\frac{700,000}{3,500.000} = \frac{1}{5} = 20\%$$

**19. (4)** maintenance of buildings

$\frac{1}{7} \times = \$3,500,000 = \$500,000$

**20. (3)** $35,000,000

$$\frac{3,500,000}{10\% \times W} = \frac{3,500,000}{.10} = 35,000,000$$